NOW IS THE TIME
TO SET THE RECORD STRAIGHT!

Cal Ripkin, Jr., Babe Ruth, Jerry Rice, Joe Montana, Michael Jordan, Wayne Gretzky, Gordie Howe, Muhammad Ali, George Foreman, Carl Lewis, Steffi Graf, Mark Spitz, Eric Heiden . . .

Winners all, what they and the hundreds of other superstars have in common in this revised and updated fourth edition of *The Illustrated Sports Record Book* is a special record (or several). Covering a broad range of sports, their history-making marks have set a standard to shoot at—and for you to use as a guide when watching your favorite sport.

THE
ILLUSTRATED
SPORTS RECORD BOOK

THE ILLUSTRATED SPORTS RECORD BOOK

by Zander Hollander and David Schulz

UPDATED AND REVISED
FOURTH EDITION

AN ASSOCIATED FEATURES BOOK

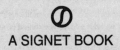

A SIGNET BOOK

SIGNET
Published by the Penguin Group
Penguin Books USA Inc., 375 Hudson Street, New York, New York 10014, U.S.A.
Penguin Books Ltd, 27 Wrights Lane, London W8 5TZ, England
Penguin Books Australia Ltd, Ringwood, Victoria, Australia
Penguin Books Canada Ltd, 10 Alcorn Avenue, Toronto, Ontario, Canada M4V 3B2
Penguin Books (N.Z.) Ltd, 182–190 Wairau Road, Auckland 10, New Zealand

Penguin Books Ltd, Registered Offices:
Harmondsworth, Middlesex, England

First published by Signet, an imprint of Dutton Signet,
a division of Penguin Books USA Inc.

First Printing, September, 1975
First Printing (Fourth Edition), October, 1996
10 9 8 7 6 5 4 3 2

Cover photo credits: Wayne Gretzky (Bruce Bennett); Michael Jordan (Wide World);
Cal Ripkin (Focus on Sports); Steffi Graf (Focus on Sports); Emmitt Smith (Focus on
Sports)

 REGISTERED TRADEMARK — MARCA REGISTRADA

Printed in the United States of America

BOOKS ARE AVAILABLE AT QUANTITY DISCOUNTS WHEN USED TO PROMOTE PRODUCTS
OR SERVICES. FOR INFORMATION PLEASE WRITE TO PREMIUM MARKETING DIVISION,
PENGUIN BOOKS USA INC., 375 HUDSON STREET, NEW YORK, NY 10014.

ACKNOWLEDGMENTS

We acknowledge with appreciation the many individuals from the professional teams, leagues, colleges and other sports organizations who helped verify the records and fill in missing information.

Countless sources were used, including eyewitnesses, newspapers and the wire services.

Z.H. and D.S.

CONTENTS

PRO FOOTBALL

PRO BASKETBALL

HOCKEY

BOXING

COLLEGE FOOTBALL

COLLEGE BASKETBALL

TRACK and FIELD

GOLF

TENNIS

HORSE RACING

AUTO RACING

SWIMMING

CYCLING

SPEED SKATING

SOCCER

BOATING

SLED-DOG RACING

INTRODUCTION

They said it couldn't be done. Who could ever break Lou Gehrig's record of 2,130 consecutive games? Cal Ripken, Jr., that's who. He did in 1995.

Records, the maxim goes, are made to be broken. Are any of them safe? Yes. Nobody will ever surpass Hoss Radbourne's 60 pitching triumphs in a single season or Ernie Nevers' 40 points in an NFL game.

But don't ever rule out Joe DiMaggio's 56 consecutive-game hitting streak, Joe Malone's seven goals in an NHL game and UCLA's 88-game winning streak in college basketball.

These are some of the vintage marks that have stood the test of time and assault by the modern superstars and super teams. But more and more athletes—faster, stronger and inspired by the glitter of gold—keep whittling away at the old standards.

This is dramatically evidenced by the fact that this revised and updated fourth edition of *The Illustrated Sports Record Book* contains more than 60 new stories with records that have been set since the third edition was published in 1991.

They are among the more than 200 stories and more than 400 records in this collection, which re-creates the feats at the time of achievement.

The record-setters are a mix of the stars of yesteryear and today—baseball's Nolan Ryan, Babe Ruth, Ken Griffey, Jr., Hank Aaron, and Bob Gibson; pro football's Jerry Rice, Jimmy Brown, Joe Montana, Walter Payton, Emmitt Smith, Fran Tarkenton, and Dan Marino; pro basketball's Michael Jordan, Wilt Chamberlain, John Stockton, Kareem Abdul-Jabbar, and Isiah Thomas;

hockey's Wayne Gretzky, Gordie Howe, Mario Lemieux, and Brett Hull; golf's Tiger Woods, Jack Nicklaus, and Bobby Jones; boxing's Muhammad Ali and George Foreman; along with such other notables in the record-smashing world as Mark Spitz, Ty Detmer, Sheryl Swoopes, Alonzo Mourning, Al Oerter, Carl Lewis, Sergei Bubka, Rod Laver, Martina Navratilova, Steffi Graf, Pete Sampras, Julie Krone, Bill Shoemaker, and Eric Heiden.

They represent only a partial listing of a cast of hundreds whose records were alive and well at the publication deadline.

Zander Hollander and David Schulz

BASEBALL

Iron Hoss

NEW YORK, Oct. 27, 1884—Pitching for the third day in a row, as he has done so often during the season, Charley "Hoss" Radbourn hurled his third successive victory today in leading the National League champion Providence Grays to a clean sweep in their playoff with the New York Metropolitans, American Association champions.

The sweep climaxed a phenomenal season for Radbourn, in which he won 60 games and lost 12 while Providence was racking up a 84–28 record. Using an overhand delivery which begins with a running start, Radbourn led the league with 441 strikeouts, a 1.38 earned-run average, 73 complete games in 75 starts, and $678\frac{2}{3}$ innings pitched. In 15 of the games in which he didn't pitch, he was in the outfield, from where he could be called to the mound if necessary. Substitutions are not allowed, even for pitchers, once the game is under way.

The 29-year-old Radbourn was not even the team's starting pitcher at the beginning of the season, but took over after Charley Sweeney was dismissed for insubordination. Radbourn's success—which included 18 straight victories during one stretch—was not without agonizing effort. When he woke up in the morning, Hoss couldn't even raise his right arm high enough to comb his hair. In order to warm up for a game, he would arrive at the field two hours before the rest of the team and start throwing, his pitches going only a few feet at first. When his teammates arrived,

Radbourn would be standing on second base ready to peg the ball home.

Most victories, season: 60, Charles Radbourn, Providence (NL), 1884

The Kid Shoots for Seven

BALTIMORE, Md., Sept. 27, 1897—People came from miles around to see the showdown. There were 3,000 men on the rooftops, plus 500 or so who hopped on and off the fences, depending upon the proximity of constables. And inside the ballpark today, 25,390 paid for the privilege of seeing the Bostons and Baltimores battle. Another 1,000 were inside the gates *gratis,* gaining access when a bleacher gate gave way under the crush of the crowd.

The showdown came, as expected, and The Kid won. Charles A. "Kid" Nichols, as nifty a righthander as baseball has seen, picked up his 30th victory of the season, giving him a record seven consecutive 30-win seasons. But what was more important to The Kid was that it was the second time in this three-game series that he had pitched a victory against the Orioles. This gave Boston a game-and-a-half lead over the defending champions in the National League pennant race.

It wasn't one of Nichols' better efforts, although he did extend his record. He gave up 13 hits, three walks, and hit an Oriole as Boston won, 19–10. The Kid had a little offensive punch of his own, getting three hits, including one in the seventh inning when Boston rallied for nine runs and put the game out of reach.

Most seasons 30 or more victories: 7, Charles A. Nichols, Boston (NL), 1891–97

Rubber Arm

CHICAGO, Ill., Oct. 6, 1908—The White Sox called on Ed Walsh for the fourth game in a row, but the big righthander didn't have anything left today as Detroit went on to win the game, 7–0, and clinch the American League pennant.

Walsh, who had a 39–15 record in 66 games this season, came on in relief after Detroit jumped on Guy White in the first inning. Before Walsh could retire the side, Detroit had a 4–0 lead. The $3^2/_3$ innings Walsh pitched raised his season's total to 464, a modern record.

Walsh had pitched Chicago into contention, winning a complete-game victory, 6–1, over Detroit yesterday to pull his team to within one-half game of the Tigers. In the game before that, Walsh recorded his seventh save of the season as he came in with the bases loaded late in the game to preserve a 3–2 victory over Cleveland. Four days ago, also against Cleveland, Walsh pitched a four-hitter, struck out 15, and walked only one, but lost, 1–0, as Addie Joss hurled a perfect no-hit, no-run game against the White Sox.

In addition to innings pitched, games, victories, and saves, Walsh led the AL with 269 strikeouts, 42 complete games, and 11 shutouts.

Most innings pitched, season (since 1900): 464, Edward A. Walsh, Chicago (AL), 1908

Cy Young's Last Game

BROOKLYN, N.Y., Oct. 6, 1911—The Brooklyn Superbas drove Cy Young off the mound and into retirement with an eight-run barrage in the seventh inning of today's game with the Boston Rustlers.

Denton True "Cy" Young, holder of the major league records for both most-games-won and most-games-lost, was touched for eight straight hits and eight runs in the second game of a doubleheader at Washington Park. After Brooklyn's Bob Coulson doubled, Young threw his glove down in disgust and walked off the mound. The Superbas had broken up a 3–3 tie when pinch hitter Zack Wheat singled home

Cy Young won 511 games.   *UPI*

Otto Miller, who had tripled. The floodgates were open
and Brooklyn went on to rout the team with the worst
record in the National League, 13–3.

Young, 44 years old and fat, finished the year with
four wins and five losses in the National League, to go
with the 3–4 record he compiled with Cleveland in the
AL earlier this season. It was the 315th defeat in his
22-year career, and goes with his 511 victories, both
totals unapproached by anyone else. Young is the only
man to win 200 or more games in each league, playing
with Cleveland and Boston in the American League between 1901 and the middle of this season. He won 222
games during that period. Young broke into the major
leagues with Cleveland in 1890, when that city had a
National League franchise. He also played with St.

Louis in addition to his brief stint with the Rustlers this season.

Before the season even began, Young indicated his desire to quit playing. He was trying to lose weight at Hot Springs, Ark., while avoiding spring training, a ritual he had long detested. It was there that he made his annual retirement announcement. This time he meant it.

Most games started, career: 818, Denton "Cy" Young, Cleveland (NL), 1890–98; St. Louis (NL), 1899–1900; Boston (AL), 1901–08; Cleveland (AL), 1909–11; Boston (NL), 1911

Most complete games, career: 751, Denton "Cy" Young, Cleveland (NL), 1890–98; St. Louis (NL), 1899–1900; Boston (AL), 1901–08; Cleveland (AL), 1909–11; Boston (NL), 1911

Most games won, career: 511, Denton "Cy" Young, Cleveland (NL), 1890–98; St. Louis (NL), 1899–1900; Boston (AL), 1901–08; Cleveland (AL), 1909–11; Boston (NL), 1911

Most games lost, career: 315, Denton "Cy" Young, Cleveland (NL), 1890–98; St. Louis (NL), 1899–1900; Boston (AL), 1901–08; Cleveland (AL), 1909–11; Boston (NL), 1911

Instant Major Leaguers

PHILADELPHIA, Pa., May 18, 1912—The crowd of 20,000 thought the game was a joke, the Philadelphia players loved the batting practice, and pitcher Aloysius Travers worked his way into the record book.

With the regular Detroit players on strike, the team's management faced a stiff fine from the league if nine players were not in uniform for today's game. The major league team that was on the field in Detroit uniforms turned out to be several members of the St. Joseph's College team, other assorted amateurs, and a couple of former big-leaguers on the Detroit executive payroll.

The regular Detroit players had warmed up before the game, then refused to take the field. They were protesting the suspension of Ty Cobb by American League president Ban Johnson after Cobb had climbed into the stands to go at it with a fan who had been riding him particularly hard in New York three days ago.

It took only an hour and 55 minutes for Philadelphia to bang out 25 hits off Travers, score 24 runs, and steal eight bases. The final score was 24–2. Travers, a former star on the St. Joseph's team, went the full eight innings and received little fielding support from his mates, who committed nine errors. Offensively, Detroit managed four hits, which produced the two runs. Each recruit picked up $50 for his efforts.

Most runs allowed by a pitcher, game: 24, Aloysius Travers, Detroit (AL), May 18, 1912

Rube Marquard of the New York Giants won 19 straight games in 1912. *UPI*

Rube the Great

CHICAGO, ILL., July 8, 1912—He knew it wouldn't last. New York Giant pitcher Rube Marquard had opened the season with a victory over Brooklyn. He won his next game, too. And the one after that. It kept going that way through April, May, and June. Five days ago, on July 3, at the Polo Grounds in New York, Marquard gave up nine hits, five walks, and had to deal with men on base in every inning but one. His team-mates worked only four hits off Napoleon Rucker, but the Giants managed to squeak by Brooklyn with a 2–1 victory, giving Rube his 19th consecutive triumph.

He hadn't lost a game and the season was nearly half over. The victory tied him with Tim Keefe of the old New York team who, back in 1888, had the advantage of pitching from much closer to the plate.

Chicago pitcher Jimmy Lavender came into today's duel with Marquard riding a modest streak of his own: 34 consecutive innings of shutout pitching. The Giants ended that string in the third inning, but Lavender had the last laugh as the Cubs scored six runs off Marquard in six innings before the Giant lefty was lifted for a pinch hitter. Heinie Zimmerman and Joe Tinker led the Chicago attack and the team played errorless ball in support of Lavender. The Cub hurler yielded only five hits as Chicago ended Marquard's skein with a 6–2 victory.

Most consecutive games won, start of season: 19, Richard W. "Rube" Marquard, New York (NL), April 11–July 3, 1912

Triple Threat

CINCINNATI, Ohio, Oct. 6, 1912—Pittsburgh center-fielder John Owen "Chief" Wilson rapped out a single and a triple today to lead a 19-hit attack in a 16–6 victory over Cincinnati. For Wilson, who finished the season with a .304 batting average, the triple was his 36th of the season, an all-time major league record for three-base hits.

The native of Austin, Tex., has been hitting the ball well all season and has used his speed to stretch many a double into a triple. Earlier this year he set a major league record by hitting six triples in five consecutive games between June 17 and June 20.

Most triples, season: 36, J. Owen Wilson, Pittsburgh (NL), 1912
Most triples, five consecutive games: 6, J. Owen Wilson, Pittsburgh
(NL), June 17–20, 1912

Pittsburgh's J. Owen "Chief" Wilson hit 36 triples in 1912.   *UPI*

The New York Giants' Christy Mathewson pitched four World Series shutouts. *UPI*

Goose Eggs in the Clutch

PHILADELPHIA, Pa., Oct. 8, 1913—Christy Mathewson singled home the first run of the game today as the New York Giants went on to beat Philadelphia, 3–0, and tie the World Series at one game each. The shutout was Mathewson's first in this series, and with the three he pitched in the 1905 Series against these same Athletics, it gives him the all-time record of four shutouts in World Series competition.

In winning today, Mathewson gave up eight hits, walked one, struck out five, and was hurt by two errors, one of which almost cost him the shutout.

Amos Strunk led off the ninth with a single and Jack Barry followed with a sacrifice bunt. Larry Doyle made a throwing error on the bunt, and the A's had men on second and third with none out. Hooks Wiltse, substituting for the injured Fred Merkle at first, made a sensational stop of a smash by Johnny Lapp and threw out Strunk at the plate. With Barry on third, pitcher Eddie Plank sizzled another one at Wiltse, who again threw home, and Barry was tagged out in a rundown. Danny Murphy then grounded out, pitcher to first, to end the game.

The 33-year-old Mathewson thus went into the record book again, adding another line to go with his modern NL mark of 37 victories in 1908 and his record of 11 seasons pitching 300 or more innings.

Most games won, season, National League (since 1900): 37, Christy Mathewson, New York (NL), 1908
World Series:
Most shutouts, career: 4, Christy Mathewson, New York (NL), 1905 (3) and 1913 (1)

A Ton of Triples

DETROIT, Mich., Sept. 22, 1916—Sam "Wahoo" Crawford, the greatest triples-hitter baseball has ever known, stroked the 312th three-bagger of his career today to spark Detroit to a 6–5 victory over Washington.

Though overshadowed by teammate Ty Cobb when it comes to public acclaim, Crawford has had some distinctions, such as being the only man ever to lead each major league in home runs. In addition, the lefthanded-hitting outfielder shares the American League's single-season record for triples with 26, hit in 1914.

Despite his proclivity for hitting triples, Crawford

has never hit two in one inning or four in one game, achievements which would have earned him another line in the record book.

A native of Wahoo, Neb., Crawford broke into the majors with Cincinnati in 1899, where he led the National League in home runs in 1901 with 16. He came to Detroit in 1903 and led the AL sluggers with seven home runs in 1908.

Most triples, career: 312, Sam Crawford, Cincinnati (NL), 1899–1902; Detroit (AL), 1903–1917

Detroit's Sam "Wahoo" Crawford stroked 312 career triples.   *UPI*

Streaking Giants

NEW YORK, Sept. 30, 1916—There was good news and bad news for the 38,000 fans who showed up at the Polo Grounds today. The good news was that Rube Benton pitched a one-hitter as the Giants beat Boston, 4–0, to extend their record winning streak to 26 games. The bad news was that Boston won the second game of the doubleheader, 8–2, to snap the streak.

The loss came as Rabbit Maranville turned in one fielding gem after another at shortstop in support of George Tyler's pitching in the nightcap. The death knell for the streak was sounded in the seventh inning when the Braves scored five runs. The key blows were back-to-back home runs by Carlisle "Red" Smith and Sherry Magee off the Giant's Slim Sallee.

Despite the streak, today's loss eliminated the Giants from the pennant race.

Most consecutive victories: 26, New York (NL), Sept. 7–30, 1916

Mr. 000 000 000

PHILADELPHIA, Pa., Oct. 2, 1916—"Alexander the Great" is what they are calling Grover Cleveland "Pete" Alexander today after the 29-year-old righthander hurled a record 16th shutout for his 33rd victory of the season. Pitching in the hitters' paradise called Baker Bowl, Alexander has had only 11 losses for the Phillies.

In today's 2–0 triumph, Pete scattered three singles among Boston hitters and allowed no runner to get past second base, as he gave up no walks and struck out four. A 4–1 loss in the second game of the doubleheader dimmed the record-book performance by Alexander, since it kept Philadelphia one game behind league-leading Brooklyn.

For the purists, Alexander's feat is only a modern record, since back in 1876 George Bradley was credited with 16 shutouts for St. Louis. But he was pitching from the old 50-foot distance rather than the modern 60-foot, 6-inch range.

Most shutouts, season: 16, Grover C. Alexander, Philadelphia (NL), 1916

A pitcher before he became a legendary home-run hitter, Babe Ruth of the Boston Red Sox hurled the most innings in a World Series game. *UPI*

Babe on the Mound

BOSTON, Mass., Oct. 9, 1916—Boston pitcher George Herman "Babe" Ruth gave up a first-inning home run to Hi Myers and held Brooklyn to only six hits in 14 innings today as Boston took a 2–0 lead in the World Series with a 2–1 triumph. In going the distance, Ruth established a record for most innings pitched in a World Series game.

Ruth struck out three and walked three as Brooklyn left five men on base. This was the first Series victory for the lefthanded Ruth, who compiled a 23–12 record during the regular season while leading the American League with nine shutouts and a 1.75 earned-run average, a record low for a lefthanded pitcher.

World Series:
Most innings pitched, game: 14, George H. "Babe" Ruth, Boston (AL), Oct. 9, 1916

On and On and On and On and

BOSTON, Mass., May 1, 1920—Communist-inspired May Day riots were the rule of the day in most major cities (three persons were killed in riots in Paris), but here in Boston the activity was much more restrained. For a record 26 innings, the Brooklyn Robins and Boston Braves sparred in an effort to win a baseball game before a chilled crowd of about 2,000. When it became too dark to play, the score was still tied, 1–1, as it had been at the end of every inning since the sixth.

Pitchers Joe Oeschger for Boston and Leon Cadore for Brooklyn went the entire distance, with Oeschger having somewhat the better of it by allowing only nine hits, including one that led to a Brooklyn run in the fifth inning. The Braves rapped 15 hits off Cadore, but could pick up only one run, in the home half of the sixth.

Only twice did it look as though the game might have a decisive outcome. In the ninth, Boston filled the bases with one out, but Charlie Pick grounded to Ivy Olson, who tagged Ray Powell on the basepath and threw to first in time to double the batter. End of threat.

Boston had a scare in the 17th inning when Oeschger allowed two hits in one inning for the only time in the game.

The bases were full of Robins when Rowdy Elliot knocked the ball back to the mound. Oeschger threw home to force Zack Wheat, but the relay to first was fumbled by Walt Holke. The first baseman retrieved the ball and whipped it home in time for catcher Hank Gowdy to tag Ed Konetchy, trying to score from second on the play.

Most innings pitched, game: 26, Leon J. Cadore, Brooklyn (NL), May 1, 1920, and Joseph C. Oeschger, Boston (NL), May 1, 1920
Most consecutive scoreless innings pitched, game: 21, Joseph C. Oeschger, Boston (NL), May 1, 1920
Most batsmen faced, game: 97, Leon J. Cadore, Brooklyn (NL), May 1, 1920
Longest game in innings: 26, Brooklyn vs. Boston (NL), May 1, 1920

Joe Oeschger was the Boston Braves' pitcher for all 26 innings of a marathon game.   *UPI*

Sizzling Sisler

ST. LOUIS, Mo., Oct. 3, 1920—George Sisler won the battle of St. Louis today, battering the scandal-scarred Chicago White Sox for three hits in a 16–7 victory for the Browns.

Sisler, the former University of Michigan athlete, showed he was as adroit with the bat as he is with a glove, finishing the season with a record 257 hits and a .407 batting average. He was also among the leading fielders in the league, topping them all in assists by a first baseman.

Sisler far outdistanced the National League's leading batter, Rogers Hornsby of the crosstown Cardinals, who wound up hitting .370 for the season. Playing in 154 games, Sisler scored 137 runs this season in 631 times at bat.

Revelations of the 1919 World Series scandal came out this year, and were followed by charges that some White Sox players had dumped this season's pennant. But the way they played today it didn't look as though the White Sox were good enough to throw anything, as the Browns pounded out 18 hits in the assault.

Most hits, one season: 257, George H. Sisler, St. Louis (AL), 1920

End of the Line

WASHINGTON, D.C., Sept. 21, 1927—The Big Train made his last stop today, running out of smoke in the fourth inning against the St. Louis Browns. If Walter Johnson's fastball wasn't what it once was, his competitive spirit remained intact.

Recovering from a broken leg sustained in spring training, Johnson worked hard to achieve a 5–5 record in his final season. Today's game didn't figure in it, since Washington came back to win, 10–7, after Walter left the mound with one out in the fourth inning. He also missed a chance to add to his record total of 113

George Sisler of the St. Louis Browns rapped 257 hits in one season. *UPI*

Washington's Walter Johnson recorded 3,508 strikeouts and notched 113 shutouts. *UPI*

career shutouts. But Johnson did strike out two Browns, to raise his major league record total to 3,508.

Johnson came into the major leagues after earning a reputation in the semipro Snake River Valley League, striking out 166 batters in 11 games as a teenager. He went directly to Washington, and, disdaining the over-hand pitching style favored by most speedballers, showed he could throw smoke from a motion somewhere between sidearm and three-quarter-arm delivery.

Despite his brilliance, Johnson was surrounded by mediocrity and he didn't play in a World Series until 1924, well past his prime, at the age of 36. His effectiveness was not just in his blazing fastball, but in his control, too. In 1913, perhaps his best year, the Big Train won 36, lost only 7, and walked only 38 men all season in compiling an earned-run average of 1.14, a record for a righthanded pitcher.

Most strikeouts, American League, career: 3,508. Walter Johnson, Washington (AL), 1907–27
Most shutouts, career: 113, Walter Johnson, Washington (AL), 1907–27
Most American League games started: 666, Walter Johnson, Washington (AL), 1907–27
Most shutouts lost, career: 65, Walter Johnson, Washington (AL), 1907–27
Most consecutive seasons pitching for one team: 21, Walter Johnson, Washington (AL), 1907–27
Most American League games won: 416, Walter Johnson, Washington (AL), 1907–27
Most American League games lost: 279, Walter Johnson, Washington (AL), 1907–27
Most innings pitched, one league: 5,924, Walter Johnson, Washington (AL), 1907–27
Most hit batsmen, career: 206, Walter Johnson, Washington (AL), 1907–27
Most batters faced, one league, career: 23,433, Walter Johnson, Washington (AL), 1907–27

Cobb's Corner

NEW YORK, Sept. 11, 1928—A crowd of 50,000 was on hand in Yankee Stadium to see an historic moment in baseball. They watched the defending World Champion New York Yankees defeat Philadelphia, 5–3, and extend their lead to 2½ games over the Athletics. The margin of victory was provided in the bottom of the eighth inning when, with Lou Gehrig on second, Babe Ruth smashed a home run off Lefty Grove.

Ty Cobb wound up with a .367 career batting average.   *UPI*

But the historic moment came in the top of the ninth inning when Ty Cobb was sent up to pinch-hit for third baseman Jimmy Dykes. The 42-year-old Georgia Peach popped a fly ball past third that was gathered in by shortstop Mark Koenig. It was Ty Cobb's last time at bat in the major leagues.

The inauspicious swan song didn't damage Cobb's average very much, for he had 114 hits in 353 times at bat this season for a healthy .323 average. And it in no way diminished his career totals, which included a record .367 lifetime batting average, only one of his many major league marks.

Highest batting average, career: .367, Tyrus R. Cobb, Detroit (AL), 1905–26, Philadelphia (AL), 1927–28

Most seasons leading major leagues in batting: 12, Tyrus R. Cobb, Detroit (AL), 1907–15, 1917–19

Most consecutive seasons leading major leagues in batting: 7, Tyrus R. Cobb, Detroit (AL), 1909–15

Most seasons batting .300 or better: 23, Tyrus R. Cobb, Detroit (AL), 1905–26, Philadelphia (AL), 1927–28

Most seasons leading American League in hits: 8, Tyrus R. Cobb, Detroit (AL), 1907–09, 1911–12, 1915–17, 1919

Most hits, American League, career: 4,191, Tyrus R. Cobb, Detroit (AL), 1905–26, Philadelphia (AL), 1927–28

Most games, five or more hits: 14, Tyrus R. Cobb, Detroit (AL), 1905–26, Philadelphia (AL), 1927–28

Most singles, American League, career (since 1900): 3,052, Tyrus R. Cobb, Detroit (AL), 1905–26, Philadelphia (AL), 1927–28

Most times stolen home: 54, Tyrus R. Cobb, Detroit (AL), 1905–26, Philadelphia (AL), 1927–28

Most runs scored, career: 2,244, Tyrus R. Cobb, Detroit (AL), 1905–26, Philadelphia (AL)

Ruthian Feat

ST. LOUIS, Mo., Oct. 9, 1928—Playing hurt and to the accompaniment of boos, hisses, jeers, and a few bottles from the leftfield stands, Babe Ruth continued his torrid hitting by swatting three home runs today to lead the New York Yankees to a 7–3 World Series victory over St. Louis.

The home runs accounted for Ruth's only runs batted in during the Series as the Yankees swept all four games. Ruth's 10 hits in 16 times at bat gave him a .625 batting average and a record 22 total bases. The Cardinal pitchers—Billy Sherdel, Grover Cleveland Alexander, Jesse Haines, Syl Johnson—could do nothing with the Babe as the Yankees won the first two games in New York, 4–1 and 9–3, before taking the pair here by identical 7–3 scores.

Ruth's three home runs, the second time he has accomplished this feat in a World Series game, helped the Yanks to a team-record nine for the Series. Lou Gehrig, who also clouted a circuit blast today, had four round-trippers in the Series, tying the Babe's 1926 mark. Thanks to the Bambino being on base so often,

Gehrig, who followed him in the batting order, drove in nine runs, a record for a four-game series.

Ruth played the entire Series with a bum knee, but the injury didn't prevent him from bringing the caterwauling fans in the stands to near silence when he made a spectacular one-handed, knee-sliding grab of a fly ball to end the game and the Series.

World Series:
Most total bases, four-game series: 22, George H. "Babe" Ruth, New York (AL), 1928

Hack Performance

CHICAGO, Ill., Sept. 28, 1930—In an era when American Leaguers are dominating the hitting statistics, Chicago Cub centerfielder Lewis "Hack" Wilson drove in two runs with a pair of singles in today's season finale to push his RBI total to a record 190 for the season as the Cubs outslugged Cincinnati, 13–11. In yesterday's game, Wilson smacked his fifty-fifth and fifty-sixth home runs of the season to establish a National League record.

Nicknamed for the popular strongman and wrestler, Hackenschmidt, Wilson is a stocky, broadfaced, no-neck righthanded batter who can hit with power. This season is the fourth time in five years that he has led the NL in home runs, and the second straight season he has driven in more than 180 runs, the only player in senior circuit history to accomplish this.

Most runs batted in, season: 190, Lewis R. "Hack" Wilson, Chicago (NL), 1930

Fence Busters

CHICAGO, Ill., Oct. 2, 1932—Murderers Row did it again, establishing offensive records left and right as the New York Yankees won their 12th consecutive World Series game today, downing the Chicago Cubs, 13–6.

As in 1927 and 1928, the Yanks were led by Babe Ruth and Lou Gehrig in sweeping their National League foes in four games. New York's team batting average of .313 is a record for a four-game series, as was Chicago's .253 for a losing team.

In addition to the team records, there were some distinctive individual performances. In yesterday's third game, for example, as Babe Ruth strode up to the plate in the fifth inning, a lemon rolled across his path. Glaring at pitcher Charlie Root, Ruth took two balls and two strikes, pointing after each pitch to a spot over the rightfield fence where he intended to hit the ball. The Babe was off in his prediction, however, as the ball sailed over the fence in dead center. Also in yesterday's game, Yankee pitcher George Pipgras struck out a record five times in five plate appearances, while the Yanks were winning, 7–5.

This was the Babe in his heyday with the Yankees. *UPI*

In today's finale, Lou Gehrig scored twice, each time on a Tony Lazzeri home run, to tie Babe Ruth's record for nine runs scored in a four-game series.

Some of the other marks established for a four-game series were one- and two-team records for times at bat, runs, hits, total bases, singles, home runs, runs batted in, walks and hit batsmen. The big hitters for the Cubs were Riggs Stephenson, Frank Demaree, Kiki Cuyler, Charlie Grimm, and Billy Herman.

World Series:
Most runs, individual, four-game series: 9, Lou Gehrig, New York (AL), 1932 (Ties George H. "Babe" Ruth, New York (AL), 1928)
Most series batting .300 or higher: 6, George H. "Babe" Ruth, New York (AL), 1921, 1923, 1926, 1927, 1928, 1932
Most strikeouts, batter, one game: 5, George Pipgras, New York (AL), Oct. 1, 1932

The Bambino Bows Out

BOSTON, Mass., June 2, 1935—As dramatic off the field as he is flamboyant on it, Babe Ruth precipitated a controversy that ended in his unconditional release today from the Boston Braves. Team president Judge Emil F. Fuchs made the decision after Ruth had attended a shipboard party in violation of curfew regulations set by manager Bill McKechnie.

The 41-year-old Ruth had been nothing more than a drawing card for the hapless Braves, wallowing in the National League cellar. Other teams in the league were holding "Babe Ruth Days" in an effort to boost attendance. A chronic knee injury had reduced the Bambino's playing time and in his last game, May 30, in Philadelphia, he played left field only briefly and failed to get a hit in his one time at bat. The day before, he settled for a pair of walks. But only a week ago, Ruth showed he was still capable of destroying pitchers.

Playing at Forbes Field in Pittsburgh, the Babe smashed three home runs off Pirate hurlers Red Lucas and Guy Bush. They were the 712th, 713th, and 714th home runs of his career, which began as a lefthanded pitcher with the Boston Red Sox in 1914.

The Sultan of Swat, Il Bambino, the Babe, or George Herman Ruth, they all started out in Baltimore, where as a seven-year-old street urchin he was sent to St. Mary's Industrial Home. He never lost the rough edge of his origins, although he won the hearts and respect of America. An early Boston teammate, Harry Hooper, recalled, "Sometimes I still can't believe what I saw, this 19-year-old kid, crude, poorly educated . . . gradually transformed into the idol of American youth and the symbol of baseball the world over."

Highest slugging average, lifetime: .690, George H. "Babe" Ruth, Boston (AL), 1914–19; New York (AL), 1920–34; Boston (NL), 1935

Most bases on balls, lifetime: 2,056, George H. "Babe" Ruth, Boston (AL), 1914–19; New York (AL), 1920–34; Boston (NL), 1935

Most seasons, 50 or more home runs: 4, George H. "Babe" Ruth, New York (AL), 1920–21, 1927–28

Most seasons 40 or more home runs: 11, George H. "Babe" Ruth, New York (AL), 1920–21, 1923–24, 1926–34

Most seasons leading major leagues in home runs: 11, George H. "Babe" Ruth, Boston (AL), 1918–19, New York (AL), 1920–21, 1923–24, 1926–29, 1931

Most seasons leading major leagues in runs scored: 8, George H. "Babe" Ruth, Boston (AL), 1919; New York (AL), 1920–21, 1923–24, 1926–28

Most seasons leading major leagues in runs batted in: 5, George H. "Babe" Ruth, New York (AL), 1920–21, 1923, 1926, 1928

Most seasons leading major leagues in slugging average: 12, George H. "Babe" Ruth, Boston (AL) 1918–19; New York (AL) 1920–21, 1923–24, 1926–31

Lefty Is Right

WASHINGTON, D.C., July 7, 1937—Vernon "Lefty" Gomez, pitching for the fourth time in the five All-Star Games that have been played, did the hurling and Yankee teammate Lou Gehrig did the hitting today as the American League beat the Nationals, 8–3, before a crowd of 31,391 that included President Franklin

Delano Roosevelt in Griffith Stadium. The victory was credited to Gomez; a record third time he has been the winning pitcher in the All-Star Game.

With Gehrig driving in four runs on a homer and a double, Gomez kept the NL at bay by allowing only one hit and walking none in his three-inning stint as starting pitcher. In 1935, Lefty worked a record six innings in the All-Star Game and allowed only three hits as the AL won, 4–1, in Cleveland. Gomez was also the winning pitcher in the first All-Star Game in 1933, which the AL won, 4–2, in Chicago.

National League starter Dizzy Dean accepted the blame for today's loss. "I shook [Gabby] Hartnett off twice and I was belted each time," Dean lamented after the game. One of those belts was a Gehrig home run that opened the AL scoring.

All-Star Game:
Most games won, lifetime: 3, Vernon "Lefty" Gomez, New York (AL), 1933, 1935, 1937

Starters in the 1937 All-Star Game: Vernon "Lefty" Gomez (left) and Dizzy Dean.   *UPI*

Detroit's Rudy York hit 18 homers in one calendar month. *UPI*

Tiger on the Loose

DETROIT, Mich., Aug. 31, 1937—Rudy York, who was sent down to the minors in June, hit his 29th and 30th home runs of the season today as the Tigers overpowered Washington, 12–3, at Navin Field.

For York, a rookie who played catcher today, the home runs brought his total for the month of August to 18, breaking by one Babe Ruth's mark of 17 homers in a calendar month, September, 1927, the year the Bambino hit 60.

In addition to the long blasts, both off Pete Appleton, York had two singles in a perfect 4-for-4 day. He drove in seven of the Tigers' 12 runs. Back on June 7, York, who was getting his second chance in the big leagues after playing briefly in 1934, had been optioned on 24-hour recall to the Toledo Mud Hens of the American Association as the Tigers called up centerfielder Chet Laabs.

Most home runs in a calendar month: 18, Rudy York, Detroit (AL), August, 1937

Dutch Treat

BROOKLYN, N.Y., June 15, 1938—There was a festive mood at Ebbets Field as a crowd of 38,748 paid to see the first major league night baseball game in the New York metropolitan area. In the stands were about 500 people from Midland Park, N.J., hometown of Johnny Vander Meer, who had pitched a no-hitter five days ago for the Cincinnati Reds against the Boston Bees.

Tonight, John's parents, his Dutch uncles and aunts and friends were on hand to present him with a gift and to watch the 23-year-old fireballer pitch against the Brooklyn Dodgers. And pitch he did. For six innings, not one Dodger got on base. Then, in the seventh inning, Vander Meer issued consecutive walks to Cookie Lavagetto and Dolph Camilli. He escaped from the inning without giving up a hit, though, and sailed through the eighth. That was 17$^1/_3$ consecutive innings of hitless pitching, topped only by the legendary Cy Young's 23 hitless frames in 1904.

With the Reds comfortably ahead, 6–0, Buddy Hassett led off the home half of the last inning by tapping the ball toward the mound. Vandy picked it up and tagged the runner on his way to first. Babe Phelps was up next and walked. Vandy's fastball had gone haywire, for he walked Lavagetto and Camilli again in

Cincinnati's Johnny Vander Meer is the only man in history to pitch back-to-back no-hitters. *UPI*

quick succession. With the bases loaded, Ernie Koy drove a hard grounder to Lew Riggs at third. Riggs was so careful fielding the ball and getting it to catcher Ernie Lombardi for the force play that there was no time for a relay and possible double play.

The bases were still full when Leo Durocher came to the plate. A deathly silence filled Ebbets Field. Durocher swung and the crowd groaned as a hard-hit ball curved foul into the rightfield stands. Durocher then lofted a short fly to centerfield which Harry Craft hauled in. Vandy had his second no-hitter in five days.

Others had pitched two no-hitters, but none had ever pitched two in one season, much less in successive games.

Most consecutive no-hitters: 2, Johnny Vander Meer, Cincinnati (NL), June 11 and June 15, 1938

Foxx Trot

ST. LOUIS, Mo., June 16, 1938—Question: How can a batter get on base six times, score two runs, and not have a time at bat?

Answer: Ask Jimmie Foxx.

Foxx, leading the American League with 19 home runs and 71 runs batted in, was issued a base on balls in each of his six plate appearances today as the Red Sox beat the St. Louis Browns, 12–8. The Boston first baseman got the passes from three St. Louis hurlers: Les Tietje, Ed Linke, and Russ Van Atta.

The six walks broke the modern mark of five in one game shared by Mel Ott of the New York Giants and Max Bishop of the Philadelphia Athletics. It also tied the pre-1900 mark of six walks set by Walter Wilmut of the Chicago Cubs in 1891.

The six plate appearances with no official time at bat duplicated the feat of Miller Huggins with the St. Louis Cardinals in 1910 and Bill Urbanski with the Boston Braves in 1934. These men did it with four walks and two sacrifices, while Charles Smith of Boston received five walks and was hit by a pitched ball back in 1890.

Most walks, game: 6, Jimmie Foxx, Boston (AL), June 16, 1938

Red Sox slugger Jimmie Foxx drew six bases on balls in one game.
UPI

All-Star Hitter

CINCINNATI, Ohio, July 6, 1938—Three National League pitchers held the American League to a lone run as the senior circuit All-Stars won the midsummer classic, 4–1, before a crowd of 27,067 today in Crosley Field.

One of the seven hits given up by the Reds' Johnny Vander Meer, the Cubs' Bill Lee and Pittsburgh's Mace Brown went to Charlie Gehringer. The Detroit second baseman, who was 1-for-3 in the game, picked up his 10th All-Star hit in 20 times at bat for a record .500 batting average.

The loss, only the second in six games for the AL, was the first in All-Star competition for Vernon "Lefty" Gomez of the Yankees, who had won three of the previous encounters.

All-Star Game:
Highest batting average (minimum 20 at-bats): .500, Charlie Gehringer, Detroit (AL), 1933–38

Thank You, Mr. Pipp

DETROIT, Mich., May 2, 1939—Batting an anemic .143 with four singles in 28 times at bat, Lou Gehrig benched himself today and thus ended the longest streak of consecutive games played since baseball began, 2,130. Gehrig was replaced by Ellsworth "Babe" Dahlgren, who hit a home run and a double as the Yankees overwhelmed the Tigers, 22–2, at Briggs Stadium.

Gehrig's decision to take himself out of the lineup was made with the approval of manager Joe McCarthy. "He'd let me go until the cows come home," Gehrig said of McCarthy. "He is that considerate of my feelings, but I knew in Sunday's game that I should get out of there." On Sunday, Gehrig was held hitless by Joe Krakauskas and Alex Carresquel as Washington beat New York, 3–2.

Lou Gehrig, with Yankee manager Joe McCarthy, benched himself after 2,130 consecutive games.   *UPI*

"It's tough to see your mates on base, have a chance to win a ball game and not be able to do anything about it," Gehrig said.

His streak began June 1, 1925, when he was sent up to pinch-hit for shortstop PeeWee Wanninger. He failed to get a hit off Walter Johnson, but was in the Yankee starting lineup the following day when regular first baseman Wally Pipp told manager Miller Huggins, "I don't feel like getting in there."

*Most seasons, 100 or more runs scored in American League: 13,
    Lou Gehrig, New York (AL) 1926–1938*
*(Editor's note: The game on April 30 marked the end of Gehrig's
    career. Gehrig was suffering from amyotrophic lateral sclerosis,
    a crippling disease, and never played baseball again. He died in
    1941.)*

Streaking Clipper

CLEVELAND, Ohio, July 17, 1941—A crowd of 67,468, the largest ever to see a major league baseball game played at night, was on hand in Municipal Stadium tonight to see whether Joe DiMaggio could extend his all-time record consecutive-game hitting streak.

The bases were full in the eighth when DiMaggio came up to face righthanded Jim Bagby, pitching in relief of lefty Al Smith. DiMag hit a 1–1 pitch on the ground and the hit was turned into a double play that ended the inning as well as his batting streak. The Yankees won, 4–3, but DiMaggio's streak was stopped after 56 games.

Most consecutive games one or more hits: 56, Joe DiMaggio, New York (AL), May 15, 1941, to July 16, 1941

Yankee clipper Joe DiMaggio hit safely in 56 consecutive games. *UPI*

Indian Courage

CLEVELAND, Ohio, July 13, 1954—Al Rosen told American League manager Casey Stengel before to-day's All-Star Game that he was willing to be dropped from the starting lineup, selected by a poll of the fans. Rosen broke a finger May 25 and the injury had been affecting his performance, but Stengel left the Cleveland infielder in the order, batting fifth and playing first base. Rosen responded by leading the AL to an 11–9 victory, giving Stengel his first victory as an All-Star manager over rookie NL pilot Walter Alston of the Brooklyn Dodgers.

Playing before a crowd of 68,751 in Municipal Stadium, three Indians treated the hometown fans to out-standing performances. Rosen hit two home runs and drove in five runs, Larry Doby clouted a pinch-hit home run and Bobby Avila went 3-for-3 and scored a run. Rosen's five runs batted in tied an All-Star record set by Ted Williams in 1946, and his two homers equaled the efforts of Williams and Pittsburgh's Arky Vaughn in 1941. Despite the bum finger, Rosen played the entire game, eight innings at first before moving to third base, replacing Detroit's Ray Boone, whose homer had provided the margin of victory for the junior circuit.

All-Star Game:
Most runs batted in, game: 5, Al Rosen, Cleveland (AL), July 13, 1954 (Ties Ted Williams, Boston (AL), July 9, 1946)

Splendid Splinter

WASHINGTON, D.C., July 10, 1956—Boston's Ted Williams and the New York Yankees' Mickey Mantle socked consecutive home runs and knocked Warren Spahn out of the box, but it still was not enough to bring victory to the American League today, as the National League won, 7–3, for the sixth time in the last seven All-Star Games.

The Red Sox' Ted Williams holds the All-Star Game career record of 12 RBI.   *UPI*

Williams, the Splendid Splinter who has been play-ing in these midsummer classics since 1940 when he hasn't been fighting in wars, homered with Chicago's Nellie Fox on base. It was Williams's first All-Star home run in 10 years. His last came in 1946 when he had a pair at Fenway Park in Boston. But the runs batted in today increased his total in All-Star Games to a record 12.

All-Star Game:
Most runs batted in, career: 12, Ted Williams, Boston (AL), 1940–56

Special Delivery

NEW YORK, Oct. 8, 1956—Using a no-windup delivery, Don Larsen of the New York Yankees retired 27 Brooklyn Dodger batters in succession today as he pitched the only perfect game in World Series history. There had never even been a no-hitter in the Series, much less a perfect one.

The 27-year-old righthander, a native of Michigan City, Ind., who grew up in San Diego, Cal., retired the final batter, pinch-hitter Dale Mitchell, with a fastball that was called strike three by umpire Babe Pinelli. The Yankees won, 2–0.

Crediting his unusual pitching motion, which is a modification of the stretch pitchers normally use with runners on base, Larsen said after the game, "It gives me better control, it takes nothing off my fastball, and it keeps the batters tense. They have to be ready every second."

There were only four near-hits Dodger batters could manage against the 6-foot 4-inch, 220-pound Larsen, who won only three games while losing 21 two seasons ago before being traded from Baltimore to the Yanks. In the second inning, third baseman Andy Carey got his glove in the way of a liner off the bat of Jackie Robinson. The ball bounced to shortstop Gil MacDougald and he pegged to first in time to nip the fleet Robinson.

In the fifth inning, Mickey Mantle made a spectacular catch in deep left center on a clout by Gil Hodges. The next batter, Sandy Amoros, hit a long drive down the rightfield line that curved foul just before going into the stands. And in the eighth inning, it was Hodges again who almost ruined Larsen's effort when he hit a low smash down the third-base line. Carey made a diving stab, but just to make sure he wasn't called for trapping it, Carey threw to first baseman Joe Collins for an unnecessary putout.

World Series:
Most consecutive batters retired, game: 27, Don Larsen, New York (AL), vs. Brooklyn (NL), Oct. 8, 1956

The Yankees' Don Larsen makes the final pitch in his perfect World Series game against the Dodgers.   *UPI*

12/13ths Perfect

MILWAUKEE, Wis., May 26, 1959—A perfect game that wasn't and a home run that was a double spelled victory for the Milwaukee Braves tonight. Pittsburgh's Harvey "The Kitten" Haddix stymied the heavy-hitting Braves, retiring a record 36 consecutive batters in 12 innings. And although Milwaukee's Lew Burdette gave up 12 hits, the Pirates failed to score in their 13 turns at bat.

Haddix, who struck out eight Braves, started the bot-

Pittsburgh's Harvey Haddix retired 36 batters in one game, but still lost. *UPI*

tom of the 13th facing Felix Mantilla, who was safe on an error by third baseman Don Hoak. Haddix's perfect game was gone, but it was still better than the 33 consecutive batters retired by Brooklyn's Ed Kimber against Toledo in 1884, back when the American

Association was a major league. And even if Haddix's perfect game was ruined, he still had a no-hitter going.

Eddie Mathews sacrificed Mantilla to second. Henry Aaron, leading the majors with a .442 batting average, was walked intentionally. This pitted lefthanded Haddix against righthanded batter Joe Adcock. The big Louisianan teed off on Haddix and parked the ball over the right-centerfield fence. Haddix was dejected, Adcock elated with the home run and the Braves' 3–0 victory, until Frank Dascoli changed the scoring. The umpire said that Aaron, who had cut across the infield after touching second base, had been passed on the baselines by Adcock, so Adcock was out. Aaron then went back, retraced his steps from second, touched third and home to score. He and Mantilla had scored the runs and the Braves won, 2–0. Adcock was given credit for a double. Haddix lost the perfect game, the no-hitter, and picked up a spectacular one-hit loss.

Most consecutive batters retired, game: 36, Harvey Haddix, Pittsburgh (NL), May 26, 1959

Men for All Ages

NEW YORK, July 13, 1960—One man many people consider too young was nominated for one job while another man who is called too old by some got a different job done today.

In Los Angeles, 43-year-old John F. Kennedy won the Democratic nomination for President, while here in Yankee Stadium 39-year-old Stan Musial hit a record sixth home run in All-Star competition to help the National League to a 6–0 victory.

Musial, who laced a pinch-hit single in this year's first All-Star Game, which the NL won, 5–3, in Kansas City two days ago, appeared again in a pinch-hitting role in the second All-Star Game of 1960. Playing in his 19th classic, Stan the Man came up in the fourth inning to bat for pitcher Stan Williams and knocked a solo blast off Gerry Staley for the Nationals' fourth

The Cardinals' Stan Musial hit six All-Star Game home runs. *UPI*

run. All of the runs were scored via homers, one each by San Francisco's Willie Mays, Milwaukee's Eddie Mathews and Musial's Cardinal teammate, Ken Boyer.

Another old-timer who was roundly cheered by the crowd was Ted Williams, six weeks short of his 42nd birthday, who singled in a pinch-hitting role for the AL.

All-Star Game:
Most home runs, career: 6, Stan Musial, St. Louis (NL), 1948–60

Driving Them In

PITTSBURGH, Pa., Oct. 12, 1960—Yankee second baseman Bobby Richardson—described by sports-writers as too good to be true—was almost too good to be believed again today as he touched Pirate pitchers for a pair of triples, drove in three runs, earned another line in the record book and, incidentally, helped New York to a 12–0 World Series triumph.

Richardson, a native of South Carolina who doesn't smoke, drink, or cuss, set a single-game record with six runs batted in during the third game of the Series, won by the Yankees, 10–0. The 25-year-old, 5-foot 9-inch, 165-pound Richardson slammed a bases-loaded home run in the first inning of that game, went 4-for-4 at the plate and drove in two more runs to eclipse the mark of five RBI shared by Yankees Bill Dickey and Tony Lazzeri, set in 1936 and equaled by Mickey Mantle in the opening game of this Series.

Today, Richardson tripled in the third inning off Tom Cheney to drive in Johnny Blanchard and Yogi Berra. These were his 10th and 11th runs batted in, surpassing the 10 RBI by Berra in 1956 and duplicated by Ted Kluszewski of the White Sox in last year's Series. Bobby upped the record to 12 when he tripled again in the seventh inning off Clem Labine, scoring Blanchard.

World Series:
Most runs batted in, series: 12, Bobby Richardson, New York (AL), 1960
Most runs batted in, game: 6, Bobby Richardson, New York (AL), Oct. 8, 1960

One Up on the Babe

NEW YORK, Oct. 1, 1961—The record that many people didn't want to see broken was broken today as New York's Roger Maris hit his 61st home run in the final game of the season off Boston Red Sox rookie Tracy Stallard. It was the 27-year-old lefthanded batter's 49th home run off a righthanded pitcher and his 30th in Yankee Stadium as he pulled a waist-high fastball on a two-strike count over the rightfield fence in the fourth inning.

Earlier in the season, baseball commissioner Ford Frick said if Maris were to break Babe Ruth's record of 60 home runs—the Babe hit his 60th on the final day of the 1927 season—it would be noted in the record book

The Yankees' Roger Maris belts his 61st home run against the Red Sox. *UPI*

with an asterisk. Frick said the difference was that Ruth played a 154-game schedule while Maris's Yankees had a 162-game schedule. Nevertheless, the two home run hitters had almost the same number of plate appearances in their record-breaking season, Ruth 692 and Maris 698. After 154 games this season, Maris had hit 59 home runs.

A crowd of 23,154 was on hand to see Maris, a native of Fargo, N.D., give the Yankees a 1–0 victory over Boston.

Most home runs, season: 61, Roger Maris, New York (AL), 1961

Yogi's String

LOS ANGELES, Cal., Oct. 5, 1963—Lawrence Peter Berra had as much trouble hitting Don Drysdale as did his Yankee teammates, and as a result the Los Angeles Dodgers won their third straight World Series game today, 1–0.

The Yankees' Yogi Berra pinch-hits against the Dodgers in his 259th World Series at-bat.   *UPI*

Berra, who has carried his childhood nickname of Yogi throughout his baseball life, was sent up to pinch-hit for pitcher Jim Bouton. Berra failed to get a hit, but his appearance extended many of his World Series records. This marked the 14th time Yogi has been in a World Series, all with the Yankees. In 75 games, he has had 259 times at bat, with 71 hits, 49 of them singles, all record totals. In addition, Berra has handled more chances and completed more putouts than any fielder at any position in World Series history.

World Series:
Most World Series: 14, L.P. "Yogi" Berra, New York (AL), 1949–53, 1955–58, 1960–63
Most games: 75, L.P. "Yogi" Berra, New York (AL), 1949–53, 1955–58, 1960–63
Most times at bat: 259, L.P. "Yogi" Berra, New York (AL), 1949–53, 1955–58, 1960–63
Most hits: 71, L.P. "Yogi" Berra, New York (AL), 1949–53, 1955–58, 1960–63

Most singles: 49, L.P. "Yogi" Berra, New York (AL), 1949–53, 1955–58, 1960–63

Most chances accepted, catcher: 457, L.P. "Yogi" Berra, New York (AL), 1949–53, 1955–58, 1960–63

Most putouts, catcher: 421, L.P. "Yogi" Berra, New York (AL), 1949–53, 1955–58, 1960–63

Changing of the Guard

ST. LOUIS, Mo., Oct. 15, 1964—Upheavals were the order of the day today. On the banks of the Moscow River a couple of guys named Brezhnev and Kosygin toppled Nikita Khruschev from power in the Soviet Union. And on the banks of the Mississippi, a couple of guys named Gibson and Brock ended the World Series reign of Mickey Mantle, Whitey Ford, and the New York Yankees.

With Bob Gibson pitching and Lou Brock hitting and stealing bases, the St. Louis Cardinals beat New York, 7–5, in the seventh and final game of the World Series. The game marked the last post-season appearances of Ford, a part-time pitching coach, who developed a sore arm in losing the opening game of the Series, and Mantle, who hit three home runs, scored eight runs, drove in eight runs, and batted .333 for the Series. Between them, they accounted for numerous records.

It was the second successive World Series loss for the Yankees. Only in 1921 and 1922, in their first two Series appearances ever, had the Yankees lost twice in a row. In between, they won 20 of the 25 Series in which they appeared.

World Series:

Most runs, career: 42, Mickey Mantle, New York (AL), 1951–53, 1955–58, 1960–64

Most extra-base hits, career: 26, Mickey Mantle, New York (AL), 1951–53, 1955–58, 1960–64

Most total bases, career: 123, Mickey Mantle, New York (AL), 1951–53, 1955–58, 1960–64

Most home runs, career: 18, Mickey Mantle, New York (AL), 1951–53, 1955–58, 1960–64

Mickey Mantle set records galore in a 65-game, 12 World Series career.   *Malcolm Emmons*

Most runs batted in, career: 40, Mickey Mantle, New York (AL), 1951–53, 1955–58, 1960–64

Most walks, career: 43, Mickey Mantle, New York (AL), 1951–53, 1955–58, 1960–64

Most strikeouts, career: 54, Mickey Mantle, New York (AL), 1951–53, 1955–58, 1960–64

World Series, pitcher:

Most series: 11, Edward C. "Whitey" Ford, New York (AL), 1950, 1953, 1955–58, 1960–64

Most games, career: 22, E.C. "Whitey" Ford, New York (AL), 1950, 1953, 1955–58, 1960–64

Most games started, career: 22, E.C. "Whitey" Ford, New York (AL), 1950, 1953, 1955–58, 1960–64

The Yankees' Whitey Ford owns many World Series marks. *UPI*

Hitting the Wind

LOS ANGELES, Cal., Sept. 9, 1965—A pair of left-handers locked horns in a pitching duel today and the result was very nearly a double no-hitter. Pitching for the hometown Dodgers was Sandy Koufax, with a flashy 21–7 record and the league lead in strikeouts with 318. Going for the Chicago Cubs was well-traveled Bob Hendley, sporting a 2–2 record.

In one of Dodger Sandy Koufax's four no-hitters, his own team got only one hit.
Malcolm Emmons

Batters were helpless against the portsiders, failing to reach base for four innings. Then, in the bottom of the fifth, the Dodgers' Lou Johnson worked Hendley for a walk, to become the first base-runner of the game. Ron Fairly sacrificed. Then Johnson stole third and, when catcher Chris Krug pegged the ball into leftfield, went on to score. Hendley lost the perfect game, the shutout, and the lead, but still had his no-hitter intact. Koufax, meanwhile, was crafting a perfect game.

The pressure was mounting and in the seventh inning, it was Johnson, again, who figured in the play. With two out, he blooped a double down the leftfield line. He was left stranded, the only man to be left on base during the entire game.

Koufax proceeded to strike out Ron Santo, Ernie Banks, and rookie Byron Browne in the eighth. He ended the game by whiffing Krug and pinch-hitters Joey Amalfitano and Harvey Kuenn.

The no-hitter, marked by his 14 strikeouts, was the fourth for Koufax, one more than the number pitched by Cy Young, Bob Feller, and Larry Corcoran.

The total of just one hit in a game is a record.

Fewest hits, both teams, one game: 1, Chicago (0) and Los Angeles (1), National League, Sept. 9, 1965

MOE-ing Them Down

LOS ANGELES, Cal., Oct. 5, 1966—Moe Drabowsky, who shares the American League record of hitting four batters in one game, pitched his way into the record books again today. Hurling for the Baltimore Orioles against the Los Angeles Dodgers in the World Series opener, Drabowsky came on in relief of Dave McNally in the third inning.

He struck out Wes Parker, forced in a run by walking Jim Gilliam, and then retired John Roseboro to quell a Dodger uprising. Drabowsky fanned a record 11 batters in all, allowed only one hit, and protected the Orioles' lead as Baltimore went on to win, 5–2.

Cast off earlier this season by Kansas City, Drabowsky started the fourth inning today by striking out pinch-hitter Jim Barbieri. Maury Wills and Willie Davis were also retired via the strikeout route. The 31-year-old Drabowsky, born in Ozanna, Poland, then proceeded to fan three more Dodgers in the fifth—Lou Johnson, Tommy Davis, and Jim Lefebvre—to tie the record of six straight set by Cincinnati's Hod Eller against the White Sox in the scandal-tainted series of

1919. The 11 strikeouts by Drabowsky, a record total for a relief pitcher, bettered the mark of 10 by Jess Barnes of the Giants against the Yankees in 1921.

Drabowsky's four hit batsmen came in a regular-season game when he was pitching for the Chicago White Sox, June 2, 1957.

World Series:
Most strikeouts by a relief pitcher: 11, Myron W. "Moe"
  Drabowsky, Baltimore (AL), Oct. 5, 1966

Frank Robinson (left), Moe Drabowsky (center), and Brooks Robinson enjoy the Orioles' 5–2 victory in the 1966 World Series opener.   *UPI*

The Mets' starting pitcher in the longest one-run shutout was Tom Seaver, who gave up two hits to the Astros before being relieved in the 10th inning. *UPI*

A Long Time Coming

HOUSTON, Tex., April 16, 1968—How long can a team go without scoring a run in one game? It took Houston 24 innings starting last night before the Astros scored a run early this morning for a 1–0 victory over the New York Mets, ending the longest one-run shutout in baseball history.

Wade Blasingame, the fifth Astros' pitcher, was the winner in a game that saw each team collect 11 hits as the Mets used eight pitchers, starting with Tom Seaver.

Here's how the winning run was scored: Norm Miller walked in the bottom of the 24th inning and advanced to second base on a balk by Met Pitcher Les Rohr. Jim Wynn was walked intentionally. Then Rusty

Staub moved the runners to second and third on an in-field out. Another intentional walk, to Hal King, loaded the bases. Houston's Bob Aspromonte then hit what looked like a double play ball, but Met shortstop Al Weis turned it into a run-scoring bobble.

Longest 1–0 game: 24 innings, New York Mets vs. Houston (NL), April 15–16, 1968

Dandy Don

HOUSTON, Tex., July 9, 1968—Willie Mays of the San Francisco Giants scored an unearned run in the first inning, but it was enough to provide the National League with a 1–0 victory and give Don Drysdale his second straight All-Star Game decision.

Starting for the fifth time in eight All-Star Games, Drysdale extended this record appearance to $19\frac{1}{3}$ innings and although he failed to fan anyone today, retained his career record of 19 strikeouts in All-Star competition.

Before the Los Angeles Dodger star displayed his mound mastery in the Astrodome, Drysdale learned that one of his regular-season records had been revised. Earlier this season he had pitched a record six straight shutouts and $58\frac{2}{3}$ scoreless innings. Today, however, the Baseball Writers Association, custodian of baseball records, said it would consider only whole innings in the record. So Drysdale will be credited with only 58 shutout innings, two more than the former record of 56 pitched by Walter Johnson in 1913.

All-Star Game:
Most innings pitched: $19\frac{1}{3}$, Don Drysdale, Los Angeles (NL), 1959–68
Most strikeouts: 19, Don Drysdale, Los Angeles (NL), 1959–68

The Dodgers' Don Drysdale pitched the most All-Star Game innings. *UPI*

All Over the Field

BLOOMINGTON, Minn., Sept. 22, 1968—Minnesota starting pitcher Cesar Tovar gave up no hits or runs, struck out one batter, walked one, and committed a balk in the first inning of tonight's game against the Oakland A's. Tovar, normally a shortstop, proceeded to play a different position each inning after that as the Twins beat Oakland, 2–1.

The first batter that Tovar faced on the mound was Bert Campaneris, who is the only other man to play all nine positions in a single major league game. He did it with the A's in Kansas City three seasons ago.

In addition to his pitching and errorless fielding, Tovar had one hit and scored a run in the Twins' triumph.

Most positions played, game: 9, Cesar Tovar, Minnesota (AL), vs. Oakland, September 22, 1968 (Ties Bert Campaneris, Kansas City (AL), vs. California Angels, Sept. 8, 1965)

Gibby's ERA

ST. LOUIS, Mo., Sept. 26, 1969—St. Louis ace Bob Gibson hurled a six-hit shutout tonight en route to compiling the lowest earned-run average in major league history. The Cardinal righthander blanked the Houston Astros, 1–0, for his 13th shutout of the season and an ERA of 1.12. Gibson's mark betters the 51-year-old record of 1.22 set by Grover Cleveland Alexander in 1917.

Curt Flood drove in Mike Shannon in the home half of the fifth inning to provide Gibson with the only run he needed, as he struck out 11 Astros to raise his league-leading total to 268. The victory was number 22, against 9 losses for Gibby as the World Series-bound Cardinals played before a crowd of 18,658.

Lowest earned-run average, season (minimum 300 innings pitched): 1.12, Bob Gibson, St. Louis (NL), 1968

Bob Gibson of the Cardinals has the record for the lowest earned-run average in a season.   *UPI*

Striking a Losing Pose

ST. LOUIS, Mo., Oct. 10, 1968—The Detroit Tigers captured the World Series by winning their third straight game today, 4–1, and not even St. Louis Cardinal strikeout king Bob Gibson could prevent it.

Gibson, who fanned a record 17 batters in the Series opener, struck out eight Tigers today in upping his World Series record total to 35. But in the end it was a game-winning rally that produced three runs in the seventh inning and gave Mickey Lolich his third victory of the Series and the Tigers the world championship.

World Series:
Most strikeouts, series: 35, Bob Gibson, St. Louis (NL), 1968
Most strikeouts, game: 17, Bob Gibson, St. Louis (NL), vs. Detroit, Oct. 2, 1968

Night All-Stars

CINCINNATI, Ohio, July 14, 1970—Despite a bipartisan start by President Richard Nixon, the first night All-Star Game ever played was an all-National League affair in Cincinnati's new Riverfront Stadium. Nixon, attending the game with daughter Julie and her husband, David Eisenhower, threw out two "first balls"— one to Cincinnati catcher Johnny Bench and one to AL starting receiver Bill Freehan of Detroit.

The Nationals scored three runs in the ninth inning and one in the 12th to defeat the Americans, 5–4, winning their eighth straight classic and their 12th in the last 13 games. The lone bright spot in the AL firmament was Boston's Carl Yastrzemski, who rapped three singles and a double in earning Most Valuable Player honors, the only thing the AL has won recently. The four hits by Yaz ties the number hit by Ducky Medwick of the Cardinals in the 1937 game and matched by Ted Williams of the Red Sox at Fenway Park in 1946.

In bringing night All-Star baseball to the city where

nighttime play was introduced to the big leagues, the Nationals won their sixth extra-inning game in six tries. The winning run scored on successive singles by the Reds' Pete Rose, Los Angeles' Billy Grabarkewitz, and Chicago's Jim Hickman.

All-Star Game:
Most hits, one game: 4, Carl Yastrzemski, Boston (AL), 1970 [Ties Joseph Medwick, St. Louis (NL), 1937; Ted Williams, Boston (AL), 1946]

The Red Sox' Ted Williams shares tips and an All-Star Game mark with Carl Yastrzemski.   *UPI*

Willie Mays played in 24 All-Star Games, setting numerous records in the process. *San Francisco Giants/SPS*

Say Hey, One More Time

KANSAS CITY, Mo., July 24, 1973—It took a special ruling from baseball commissioner Bowie Kuhn to do it, but Willie Mays played in his 24th All-Star Game. Kuhn increased the player limit for the game so that stars such as Mays and California's no-hit pitcher Nolan Ryan could be included on the All-Star rosters. As a result, there were a record 58 players selected for the squads, 54 of whom saw action tonight in the

National League's 7–1 victory in Royals Stadium, part of the new Harry S. Truman Sports Complex here.

Home runs by Cincinnati's Johnny Bench, San Francisco's Bobby Bonds, and Los Angeles' Willie Davis powered the NL to its 10th triumph in the last 11 games.

Mays, whose first 23 appearances were in a Giant uniform, was representing the New York Mets this year. And even though he was struck out by the Yankees' Sparky Lyle, who was in his first All-Star Game, Mays received a standing ovation from the crowd of 40,849.

All-Star Game:
Most at-bats: 75, Willie Mays, New York (NL), San Francisco (NL), New York (NL), 1951–73
Most runs: 20, Willie Mays, New York (NL), San Francisco (NL), New York (NL), 1951–73
Most hits: 23, Willie Mays, New York (NL), San Francisco (NL), New York (NL), 1951–73
Most singles: 15, Willie Mays, New York (NL), San Francisco (NL), New York (NL), 1951–73
Most stolen bases: 6, Willie Mays, New York (NL), San Francisco (NL), New York (NL), 1951–73

Record Relief

HOUSTON, Tex., Oct. 1, 1974—Relief pitcher Mike Marshall and his Los Angeles teammates prepared for the National League playoffs with an 8–5 victory tonight over the Houston Astros.

Marshall, who earlier this year had appeared in 13 consecutive games as a pitcher, was not particularly effective as he gave up two hits, walked six batters, and yielded four runs in the two innings he worked.

But the appearance did nothing to dim the overall season's performance of Marshall, who is pursuing a doctoral degree in kinesiology at Michigan State in the off-season. He has appeared in 106 games, shattering his own major league record of 92 set last season with the Montreal Expos. Marshall's 208 innings were also a season's record for a relief pitcher.

Most games, pitcher, season: 106, Mike Marshall, Los Angeles (NL), 1974

Most innings pitched, relief pitcher, season: 208, Mike Marshall, Los Angeles (NL), 1974

Hank Hammers No. 755

MILWAUKEE, Wis., July 20, 1976—Henry Aaron hit his 10th home run of the season and the 755th of his career tonight as he helped the Milwaukee Brewers defeat the California Angels, 6–2.

The 42-year-old Aaron, who came into the game batting just .247 as a part-time player, has had questions of retirement swirling around him since the season began. He has been playing in Milwaukee since the beginning of last season after being released by the Atlanta Braves, returning to the city in which he began his major league career in 1954 with the then Milwaukee Braves of the National League.

Of course, of all his home runs in a 23-year career, none was more memorable than the one he hit on April 8, 1974, in Fulton County Stadium as a member of the Atlanta Braves.

As he, and anyone else who was watching, recalls the scene, Los Angeles Dodgers' pitcher Al Downing went into a stretch, looked the runner back to first base, and fired home. The ball was straight and true, over the plate and rising slightly along the way. Aaron swung hard, unleashing power with a last instant snap of the wrists, and the ball sailed toward the leftfield fence. Henry slowed to a trot, rounding first base as he watched the ball elude the flailing reach of Bill Buckner, who had scaled the fence to lunge at it. The crowd was hammering, hooting, stomping, and whistling approval. Two teenage boys joined Aaron on his circuit of the bases. Dodger infielders congratulated him as he went by.

Henry Aaron responds to reporters after he broke Babe Ruth's home-run record. *UPI*

That was the 715th time Henry Aaron had hit a home run in a regular-season major league game, and it was the blast that moved Aaron to the top of the heap, ahead of Babe Ruth as the all-time leading hitter of home runs.

Today's 755th came off a pitcher named Mickey Scott in a game between two last-place teams.

Most home runs, career: 755, Henry Aaron, Milwaukee (NL), 1954–65; Atlanta (NL), 1966–74; Milwaukee (AL), 1975–76

Mr. October

NEW YORK, Oct. 18, 1977—Reggie Jackson capped his first season as a New York Yankee by blasting three home runs to give the Bronx Bombers an 8–4 vic-

Reggie Jackson powers his third home run as the Yankees win the game, 8–4, as well as the World Series, against the Dodgers in 1977.   *UPI*

tory over the Los Angeles Dodgers as they won their first World Series in 15 years.

The flamboyant Jackson, who signed a multimillion-dollar free-agent contract with the Yankees after playing in Baltimore last season, was a controversial figure during the season, often feuding with manager Billy Martin and sometimes with his teammates in the dugout.

All that was forgotten tonight as he smacked the first pitch out of the park in three consecutive times at bat, driving in four runs. He also walked once and scored four times.

In his last nine times at bat in the six-game series, the 31-year-old Jackson hit five home runs, the last four in consecutive official times at bat.

World Series:
Most home runs, one series: 5, Reggie Jackson, New York (AL) 1977
Most home runs, game: 3, Reggie Jackson, New York (AL), Oct. 18, 1977 [Ties George H. "Babe" Ruth, New York (AL), Oct. 6, 1928]
Most total bases, game: 12, Reggie Jackson, New York (AL), Oct. 18, 1977 [Ties George H. "Babe" Ruth, New York (AL), Oct. 6, 1928]
Most home runs, consecutive times at bat: 4, Reggie Jackson, New York (AL), Oct. 16–18, 1977

King of Thieves

KANSAS CITY, Kan., Oct. 2, 1982—Rickey Henderson of the Oakland A's stole his 128th, 129th, and 130th bases of the season here today, and that's more than anyone has recorded since the 19th century when runners were credited with a stolen base for going from first to third on a single.

The stolen bases were in a losing cause as the A's lost to the Kansas City Royals, 5–4. But the victory didn't do much good for the second-place Royals either, since the California Angels won today and clinched the divisional pennant.

The 5-foot 10-inch, 180-pound Henderson, who was born on Christmas Day, 1958, in Chicago, had eclipsed Lou Brock's former modern record of 118 stolen bases more than a month ago, but injuries have reduced his playing time since then. All of his base running this season earned Henderson another major league record. He was caught stealing 42 times, an all-time high.

Most stolen bases, season (since 1900): 130, Rickey Henderson, Oakland (AL), 1982
Most times caught stealing, season: 42, Rickey Henderson, Oakland (AL), 1982

This was the steal by Rickey Henderson of the A's that broke Lou Brock's record of 118 stolen bases.   *UPI*

Gooden Plenty

NEW YORK, Nov. 13, 1985—Dwight Gooden, three days short of his 21st birthday, today became the youngest player ever to win the Cy Young Award, emblematic of the best pitcher in the league.

The New York Met righthander was a unanimous choice for his performance this year, his second in the major leagues, which included 24 victories against 4 losses and a 1.53 earned-run average in 276 $^2/_3$ innings pitched. Gooden struck out 268 batters while walking 69 and allowing 51 runs, 47 of them earned.

The native of Tampa, Fla., started 35 games, completed 16, and hurled eight shutouts along the way.

Nicknamed "The Doctor" and sometimes called "Dr. K" for his strikeout proficiency, Gooden this past season led the major leagues in victories, ERA, and

Dwight Gooden of the Mets captured the Cy Young Award in 1985 to become the youngest winner ever.   *Mitchell Reibel*

strikeouts, the first man to win the so-called pitching triple crown since Sandy Koufax turned the trick in 1966.

Youngest pitcher to win a Cy Young Award: Dwight Gooden, 20 years, 362 days old, New York (NL), 1985

The Red Sox' Roger Clemens shows the game ball after his 20 strikeouts against the Mariners in 1986.　　　*Wide World*

20 Whiffs

BOSTON, Mass., April 29, 1986—Boston Red Sox righthander Roger Clemens, who underwent shoulder surgery eight months ago, today set a major league record by striking out 20 batters in a nine-inning game as the Bosox defeated the Seattle Mariners, 3–1.

The 20 strikeouts surpassed the previous record of 19 shared by Nolan Ryan of the California Angels in 1974, Tom Seaver of the New York Mets in 1970, and Steve Carlton of the St. Louis Cardinals in 1969. Only Tom Cheney of the Washington Senators has struck out more batters in a game, fanning 21 in 16 innings against Baltimore in 1962.

Along the way Clemens, who now has four victories and no defeats, struck out eight consecutive batters from the fourth to the sixth inning before Spike Owen flied to center. Clemens later struck out Owen in the ninth inning to tie the record before making Phil Bradley his 20th victim of the game.

Clemens, who had a 9–4 won-lost mark and 126 strikeouts in his rookie season two years ago, developed arm trouble last year. He had a 7–5 record pitching 98 innings with 74 strikeouts. On Aug. 30 he underwent surgery on his right shoulder and was out for the rest of the season.

Most strikeouts, nine-inning game: 20, Roger Clemens, Boston (AL), April 29, 1986

Most consecutive strikeouts, American League game: 8, Roger Clemens, Boston, April 29, 1986 (Ties Nolan Ryan, California, Aug. 7, 1973, and July 9, 1972, and Ron Davis, New York (AL), May 4, 1981)

Fernando's Screwball

HOUSTON, Tex., July 15, 1986—With his screwball working to perfection, southpaw Fernando Valenzuela of the Los Angeles Dodgers struck out five straight batters in the All-Star Game tonight, matching the record established 52 years ago by Carl Hubbell of the New York Giants. The American League went on to win the game, however, 3–2.

Hubbell, also a lefthanded screwball artist, set down Babe Ruth, Lou Gehrig, Jimmie Foxx, Al Simmons, and Joe Cronin, all future Hall of Famers, in the 1934 All-Star Game.

Valenzuela's task was somewhat less formidable as he got Don Mattingly, Cal Ripkin, and Jesse Barfield on swinging strikes in the fourth inning. He then caught Lou Whitaker looking in the fifth before getting fellow Mexican Teddy Higuera on a swinging strike. Higuera, the Milwaukee Brewer pitcher, had not batted

The Dodgers' Fernando Valenzuela tied an All-Star Game mark with his five consecutive strikeouts in 1986. *Wide World*

in a regular-season game in six years because of the designated-hitter rule.

After recording the five consecutive Ks, the 26-year-old Valenzuela had his string snapped by Kirby Puckett, who bounced out to short.

All-Star Game:
Most consecutive strikeouts: 5, Fernando Valenzuela, Los Angeles (NL), July 15, 1986 (Ties Carl Hubbell, New York (NL), July 10, 1934)

4,000 for Lefty

SAN FRANCISCO, Cal., Aug. 5, 1986—After back-to-back third-inning singles by Buddy Bell and Dave Parker put runners on first and third for Cincinnati, San Francisco's Steve Carlton got Eric Davis to swing and miss on a 3–2 fastball.

It was the 4,000th strikeout of Carlton's career, the National League record.

Little else worked right for the 41-year-old Carlton tonight as he yielded seven hits and seven runs in $3\frac{2}{3}$ innings in the Giants' 11–6 loss to the Reds. The southpaw known as "Lefty" now has a 5–14 record for a season that began with the Philadelphia Phillies.

Now in his 22nd year in a career that started in St. Louis, Carlton won the Cy Young Award a record four times with the Phillies. His most spectacular season was in 1972 when he won 27 games with an ERA of 1.97 with Philadelphia.

Most strikeouts, National League, career: 4,000, Steve Carlton, St. Louis, 1965–71; Philadelphia, 1972–86; San Francisco, 1986
Most Cy Young Awards: 4, Steve Carlton, Philadelphia (NL), 1972, 1977, 1980, 1982

The scoreboard hails the Giants' Steve Carlton after he posted his 4,000th strikeout in 1986. *Wide World*

Charlie Hustle

CINCINNATI, Ohio, Aug. 17, 1986—Cincinnati player-manager Pete Rose came in as a pinch hitter today and looked at a third strike thrown by San Diego's Goose Gossage in a 9–5 Padres' triumph.

Depending on whether he decides to concentrate solely on managing from now on, it may have been the final plate appearance for the 45-year-old native of Cincinnati.

The 5-foot-11-inch, 200-pound Rose has been reluctantly winding down since he broke Ty Cobb's career record of 4,191 base hits in Cincinnati on Sept. 11, 1985, with a single off San Diego righthander Eric Show—57 years to the day that Cobb last came to bat.

Cincinnati's Pete Rose watches the hit that broke Ty Cobb's record in 1985.   *Wide World*

In his last 10 at-bats, Rose hasn't had a hit, but just prior to that, on Aug. 14, he went 3-for-4 and drove in a run to lead the Reds to a 2–0 victory over the San Francisco Giants.

His career batting average is .303 and his many major league records are eloquent testimony to 24 years of achievement and hustle.

Most base hits, career: 4,256, Peter E. Rose, Cincinnati (NL), 1963–78; Philadelphia (NL), 1978–1983; Montreal (NL) and Cincinnati (NL), 1984; Cincinnati (NL), 1985–86
Most plate appearances, career: 15,890, Peter E. Rose
Most times on base, career: 5,958, Peter E. Rose
Most games, career: 3,562, Peter E. Rose
Most seasons 150 or more games: 17, Peter E. Rose
Most seasons 100 or more games: 23, Peter E. Rose
Most at bats, career: 14,053, Peter E. Rose
Most seasons 600 or more at bats: 17, Peter E. Rose
Most consecutive seasons 600 or more at bats: 13, Peter E. Rose
Most runs scored, National League career: 2,165, Peter E. Rose
Most seasons leading major leagues in base hits: 7, Peter E. Rose (Ties Ty Cobb)
Most singles, career: 3,215, Peter E. Rose

Canadian Bombers

TORONTO, Canada, Sept. 14, 1987—Led by Ernie Whitt's three round-trippers, the Toronto Blue Jays pounded out a record 10 home runs tonight in routing the Baltimore Orioles, 18–3.

The lefthanded-hitting Whitt got things started with a solo shot in the second, hit another bases-empty homer in the fifth and knocked a three-run blast in the seventh that was Toronto's ninth homer of the game, breaking the record of eight set by the 1939 New York Yankees and tied by six teams since then.

George Bell slammed a pair of homers to boost his major-league-leading total to 45. Rance Mulliniks also hit a pair, while Lloyd Moseby, Rob Ducey, and Fred McGriff each had one homer.

The Orioles' Mike Hart belted one out of the park in the third inning, making it 11 home runs between the two teams, tying a record set by the Yankees and Detroit Tigers in 1950 and previously equaled twice.

Most home runs, one team, game: 10, Toronto (AL), Sept. 14, 1987

Grand Grand Slam

NEW YORK, Sept. 29, 1987—Don Mattingly, who before this season had never hit a major league home run with the bases full, drove a 1–2 change-up into the right-

The Yankee's Don Mattingly was master of the grand slam.

Mitchell Reibel

field seats for his sixth grand slam of the season tonight as the New York Yankees defeated Boston, 6–0.

Four days ago, the 26-year-old first baseman hit his fifth grand slam of the season against the Baltimore Orioles, which tied him with the Chicago Cubs' Ernie Banks (1955) and the Orioles' Jim Gentile (1961) for the major league mark.

Tonight's record-setter came off Red Sox lefthander Bruce Hurst in the third inning with no score in the game. Roberto Kelly and Rickey Henderson were on base with back-to-back singles and Willie Randolph walked to fill the bases, setting the stage for Mattingly's record swing.

Back in July, Mattingly homered in eight consecutive games to tie Dale Long's 30-year-old record, and his 10 homers in that span are a record.

Most home runs with bases full, season: 6, Don Mattingly, New York (AL), 1987

Most home runs, eight consecutive games: 10, Don Mattingly, New York (AL), July 8–18, 1987

K-Meister

ANAHEIM, Calif., Sept. 30, 1989—In a game devoid of meaning from a won-lost standpoint, Texas Ranger Nolan Ryan furnished plenty of excitement as he flirted with his sixth career no-hitter and recorded a 300-strikeout season for the sixth time tonight by shutting out the California Angels, 2–0.

The Oakland A's had long since sewed up the American League West divisional title, but Ryan kept the crowd of 34,910 glued to its seats in Anaheim Stadium as he took a perfect game into the eighth inning. Brian Downing shot it down with a one-out single, which was actually greeted by boos from the Angel fans, and Dante Bichette followed up with another one-bagger.

Mark McLemore added a meaningless single in the ninth inning as Ryan struck out four of the last six batters to face him. His 12th K of the game, and 300th of the season, was shortstop Dick Schofield leading off the ninth.

There have been only 22 300-strikeout seasons in baseball, and Ryan has reached that total 6 times, including the all-time high of 383 strikeouts in 1973 when he was pitching for the Angels.

Five weeks ago, Ryan fanned Oakland's Ricky Henderson to record the 5,000th strikeout of his career, the first pitcher to reach that level.

At 42, Ryan is the oldest of the 11 pitchers to strike out 300 batters in a season, and he accomplished the feat in the fewest number of innings, just 239 this season.

Most seasons 300 or more strikeouts: 6, Nolan Ryan, California (AL), 1972–74, 1976–77; Texas (AL), 1989

The No-Hit Season

CLEVELAND, Ohio, Sept. 2, 1990—In an improbable season of no-hitters, Toronto's Dave Stieb finally earned a place in the record book today with a 3–0 no-hit victory over the Cleveland Indians here this afternoon.

Not that Stieb was an improbable candidate to pitch a no-hitter. Three times in the last two years he came within one out of pitching a no-hitter—that's more eight-and-two thirds innings no-hitters than anyone else in history.

Today, though, with two out in the home half of the ninth, Stieb walked Alex Cole on four pitches before getting Jerry Browne to line a 1–1 pitch directly at Junior Felix in right field for the final out.

It may have been Stieb's first no-hitter, but it was the seventh in the major leagues this season, tying a record.

More than a few of this season's no-hitters had an additional twist. Back on July 1, Andy Hawkins of the New York Yankees didn't give up a hit in eight innings, but lost, 4–0, to the Chicago White Sox. On

June 29, both Dave Stewart of the Oakland A's and Fernando Valenzuela of the Los Angeles Dodgers pitched no-hitters, the first time there were same-day no-hitters since 1898.

On June 11, 43-year-old Nolan Ryan recorded the sixth no-hitter of his career; on June 2, 6-foot 10-inch Randy Johnson of the Seattle Mariners became the tallest man to throw a no-hitter with a 2–0 effort against Detroit, and on April 11, California Angels' pitchers Mark Langston and Mike Witt combined for a no-hitter against the Mariners.

The other no-hitters came on Aug. 15, when Philadelphia's Terry Mulholland stymied his former teammates, the San Francisco Giants, and on July 12, when the Chicago White Sox' Melido Perez didn't yield a hit in a rain-shortened six-inning game against the Yankees.

No-hitters of less than nine innings are not considered official by Major League Baseball, so Hawkins and Perez do not get credited.

Most no-hit games, season: 7, 1990
Most no-hit games, one league, season: 5, American League, 1990
   (Ties AL, 1917)

Sox Saver

CHICAGO, Sept. 30, 1990—If it weren't for the fact that this was the last baseball game played in Comiskey Park, the White Sox' 2–1 victory over the Seattle Mariners today would probably be best remembered as the game in which Bobby Thigpen recorded his 57th save of the season.

Though they have the second-best record in the majors, the White Sox trail the division-winning Oakland A's by nine games with three left to play. A crowd of 42,849—1,082 less than capacity—was on hand to cheer the Sox for their effort and to perhaps recall highlights of the south side stadium's 80-year history.

For the 26-year-old Thigpen, an outfielder in his col-

Fireman Bobby Thigpen of the White Sox came to the rescue with 57 saves in 1990. *Vic Milton*

lege days at Mississippi State, this has been a season to remember. The right-hander has had 65 chances to save games, making good on 57 of the opportunities.

Nearly a month ago, on Sept. 3, with the White Sox still in the thick of the pennant race, Thigpen notched his 47th save in a 4–2 victory over Kansas City in

Comiskey Park. That broke the record of 46 saves set by Dave Righetti of the New York Yankees in 1986.

The 6-foot 3-inch, 195-pound Thigpen, a native of Tallahassee, Fla., had 91 saves in 200 games in his 3½ years in the major leagues prior to this season.

Most saves, season: 57, Bobby Thigpen, Chicago (AL), 1990

Hatcher's Hatch

CINCINNATI, Ohio, Oct. 17, 1990—Joe Oliver, who hit .231 in the regular season, singled in the winning run in the 10th inning tonight as the Cincinnati Reds edged the Oakland Athletics, 5–4, in Game 2 of the World Series.

Nobody can take a rare headline away from the part-time Reds' catcher—nobody except teammate Billy Hatcher, who slugged his way into the record book.

Hatcher, a 30-year-old outfielder who had never achieved singular honors in five full seasons in the majors, connected for four hits, establishing a Series record with hits in seven successive at-bats. He'd had three in a row in the Reds' 7–0 shocker of the A's in Game 1.

Hatcher broke the mark of six set by Goose Goslin of the Washington Senators in 1924 and tied by Thurman Munson of the New York Yankees in 1976.

Most consecutive hits, World Series: 7, Billy Hatcher, Cincinnati (NL), 1990
Highest batting average, one series: .750, Billy Hatcher, Cincinnati (NL), 1990

Ryan's Seven-Up

ARLINGTON, Tex., May 1, 1991—With a home crowd of 33,439 chanting "No-lan, No-lan," 44-year-old Nolan Ryan mowed down Roberto Alomar for the last out to record the seventh no-hitter of his career

Cincinnati's Billy Hatcher triples for his seventh consecutive hit against the A's in the 1990 World Series. *Wide World*

tonight as the Texas Rangers beat the Toronto Blue Jays, 3–0.

Ryan, who pitched his last no-hitter less than a year ago against the A's in Oakland, was in complete control throughout the game. Only two men reached base: Kelly Gruber, walking on a 3–2 pitch in the first inning, and Joe Carter getting a full-count base on balls in the seventh. Neither runner advanced.

The Blue Jays, who came into the game leading the

The Rangers' Nolan Ryan records his seventh no-hitter against the Blue Jays in 1991. *Wide World*

major leagues in hitting with a .276 team average, struck out 16 times during the game. It was the 26th time in his career that Ryan whiffed 15 or more batters in a game.

Ryan, whose fastball averaged 93 miles an hour tonight, threw his first no-hitter 18 years ago—May 15, 1973—for the California Angels against the Kansas City Royals.

"I had the best command of all three pitches," the future Hall of Famer said after the game. "This is the best, this is my most overpowering night."

Most no-hit games: 7, Nolan Ryan, Texas (AL), vs. Toronto (AL), May 1, 1991; California (AL), vs. Kansas City (AL), May 15, 1973; California (AL), vs. Detroit (AL), July 15, 1973; California (AL), vs. Minnesota (AL), Sept. 24, 1974; California (AL), vs. Baltimore (AL), June 1, 1975; Houston (NL), vs. Los Angeles (NL), Sept. 26, 1981; Texas (AL), vs. Oakland (AL), June 11, 1990

A 79-year-old record was tied when the Braves' Otis Nixon stole six bases in one game. *Wide World*

Made of Steal

MONTREAL, June 16, 1991—Playing against his former team, Otis Nixon of the Atlanta Braves stole six bases tonight, tying one of the oldest records in the book, but it still wasn't enough as the hometown Expos edged the Braves, 7–6.

Acquired from Montreal prior to the start of the season, Nixon leads the Braves with 32 steals. Leading off the third inning with a bunt base-hit, he stole second and third to give him four thefts at that point, setting a Braves' single-game record. Nixon singled again in the ninth inning and stole second and third, but was left stranded to end the game.

The six steals ties the modern major league record set by Eddie Collins of the Philadelphia A's in 1912 in a suspended game played on two days. George Gore of Chicago and Billy Hamilton of Philadelphia are credited with seven steals in a game, but scorekeepers in the 1880s often credited runners with a stolen base on a fielder's choice or when they stretched a hit an extra base if the fielder's throw was late or off-target.

Most stolen bases, game, since 1900: 6, Otis Nixon, Atlanta (NL), June 16, 1991 (Ties Eddie Collins, Philadelphia (AL), Sept. 11, 22, 1912)

Old-Time Swinger

BALTIMORE, Md., Sept. 24, 1992—Dave Winfield drove in four runs with a homer and a double to lead the Blue Jays past the Orioles tonight, 8–2. The victory keeps Toronto in first place, three-and-a-half games ahead of Milwaukee in the American League East.

The 40-year-old Winfield now has 103 RBI for the season and is the oldest player ever to drive in 100 runs in a season.

Oldest player with 100 or more runs batted in, season: Dave Winfield, Toronto (AL), 1992

Always Coming Up Short

LOS ANGELES, July 24, 1993—Anthony Young of the New York Mets walked home the winning run with two outs in the 10th inning to provide Los Angeles with a 5–4 victory before a crowd of 43,301 at Dodger Stadium tonight.

Young came in relief to start the eighth with the score tied, 4–4, and wound up losing his 13th straight game this season and 27th in a row over two seasons. He has not won a game, either as a starter or in relief, since May 6, 1992.

Most consecutive losses, league: 27, Anthony Young, New York (NL), May 6, 1992–July 24, 1993

Most consecutive losses from start of season, National League: 13, Anthony Young, New York (NL), April 9–July 24, 1993

Four Four-Baggers

CINCINNATI, Ohio, Sept. 7, 1993—After misplaying a ball that allowed Cincinnati to win the opener, 14–13, the Cardinals' Mark Whiten single-handedly battered the Reds in the nightcap to lead St. Louis to a 15–2 victory.

All Whiten did was slam four home runs, tying a record, and drive in 12 runs, tying another, after going hitless in the first game. Among Whiten's blasts were a grand slam off Larry Luebers in his first time at-bat, and homers in his last three trips to the plate.

The 25-year-old Whiten, who came to the Cardinals in an off-season trade with Cleveland, tied such notables as Mike Schmidt, Willie Mays, Gil Hodges, and Lou Gehrig with his four homers. The 12 RBI ties the 69-year-old mark set by the Cardinals' Jim "Boom-Boom" Bottomley Sept. 16, 1924, against the Brooklyn Dodgers.

In addition, Whiten had one RBI in the first game, giving him 13 for the doubleheader, tying a record set by San Diego's Nate Colbert in 1972.

Most home runs, game: 4, Mark Whiten, St. Louis (NL), Sept. 7, 1993 (Ties Robert T. Lowe, Boston (NL), May 30, 1894; Edward Delahanty, Philadelphia (NL), July 13, 1896; Lou Gehrig, New York (AL), June 3, 1932; Chuck Klein, Philadelphia (NL), July 10, 1936; J. Patrick Seery, Chicago (AL), July 18, 1948; Gil Hodges, Brooklyn (NL), July 31, 1954; Rocky Colavito, Cleveland (AL), June 10, 1959; Willie Mays, San Francisco (NL), April 30, 1961; Mike Schmidt, Philadelphia (NL), April 17, 1976; Bob Horner, Atlanta (NL), July 6, 1986)

Most runs batted in, game: 12, Mark Whiten, St. Louis (NL), Sept. 7, 1993 (Ties James L. Bottomley, St. Louis (NL), Sept. 16, 1924)

Most runs batted in, doubleheader: 13, Mark Whiten, St. Louis (NL), Sept. 7, 1993 (Ties Nate Colbert, San Diego (NL), Aug. 1, 1972)

King of the K's

ANAHEIM, Cal., Sept. 17, 1993—"I know I'm done. It's been a real tough year, physically and emotionally. I hurt all the time. This body's run its course. It's time to do something else."

These were the words of 46-year-old Nolan Ryan tonight after the Texas Ranger pitched seven strong innings in a 2–1 loss to the California Angels.

The game marked the finale for the nonpareil righthander whose 27 seasons in the majors are only one of many records made in a career with the New

York Mets, California Angels, Houston Astros, and Texas Rangers.

Pitching before a crowd of 60,326 at Anaheim Stadium, Ryan yielded four hits and struck out five, giving him a record career total of 5,714 strikeouts. Along the way he threw a record seven no-hitters and in 1973, with the Angels, he fanned 386 batters, the most ever in a season.

Among Ryan's most notable marks:

Most strikeouts, career: 5,714, Nolan Ryan, New York (NL) 1966, 1968–71; Houston (NL), 1980–88; California (AL), 1972–77; Texas (AL), 1989–93

Most seasons, pitching: 27, Nolan Ryan, New York (NL), 1966, 1968–71; Houston (NL), 1980–88; California (AL), 1972–77; Texas (AL), 1989–93

Most games started, consecutive: 595, Nolan Ryan (AL) California (AL), 1974–79; Houston (NL), 1980–88; Texas (AL), 1989–93

Homeric Binge

DETROIT, Mich., May 28, 1995—It was Sluggers' Day at Tiger Stadium today as the Chicago White Sox and Detroit Tigers slammed a major league record 12 home runs and an American League record 21 extra-base hits in a 14–12 victory for the visiting Chisox.

Ten of the homers were solo shots, another major league mark, while Cecil Fielder, Chad Curtis, and Kirk Gibson of the Tigers and Ron Karkovice of the White Sox each had a pair of homers for an AL record for most players with at least two home runs in a game, tying the major league record set in 1947 by the Pittsburgh Pirates and St. Louis Cardinals.

Most home runs, game, both teams: 12, Chicago (AL) vs. Detroit, May 28, 1995

Most home runs, no one on, game, both teams: 10 Chicago (AL) vs. Detroit, May 28, 1995

Most players two or more home runs, game, American League: 4, Cecil Fielder, Chad Curtis, Kirk Gibson, Detroit; Ron Karkovice, Chicago, May 28, 1995 [ties Whitey Kurowski,

Detroit's Cecil Fielder is one of four players with two homers in the same game.
Wide World

St. Louis (NL); Ralph Kiner (3), Hank Greenberg, Billy Cox, Pittsburgh, Aug. 16, 1947]
Most extra-base hits in a game, both teams: 21, Chicago (AL), 10, and Detroit, 11, May 28, 1995

To the Rescue

ARLINGTON, Tex., June 28, 1995—Texas rallied for three runs in the bottom of the ninth inning tonight to edge California, 9–8, and snap Lee Smith's streak of consecutive games saved at 19.

The hard-throwing Smith, who led the majors with 23 saves while pitching for Baltimore last season, entered the game in the eighth inning and struck out Benji Gil to preserve an 8–6 Angel lead.

It was the first time in 21 appearances this season that the 37-year-old Smith had come into a game prior to the ninth inning.

In suffering his first loss of the year, Smith walked leadoff batter Otis Nixon to start the last inning. Mark McLemore followed with a single and Will Clark's double off the center field fence tied the score at 8–all. Clark later scored the winning run on Ivan Rodriguez's single.

Eight days ago, in Anaheim, Smith had preserved a 3–2 victory over Kansas City for his 18th save in 18 appearances, breaking his own major league record of 17 straight saves set with the St. Louis Cardinals in 1993.

Most saves, consecutive games: 19, Lee Smith, California (AL), April 28—June 25, 1995

Junior's Eight Straight

SEATTLE, Wash., July 28, 1995—Ken Griffey, Jr. powered a 400-foot home run into the third deck in right field at the Kingdome tonight for Seattle's only run in a 5–1 loss to the Minnesota Twins.

Leading off in the seventh inning, Griffey victimized Twins starter Willie Banks for his 30th home run of the season. This was the eighth straight game in which Junior has homered, tying the major league record shared by Don Mattingly of the New York Yankees in 1987 and Dale Long of the Pittsburgh Pirates in 1956.

Griffey's streak started last week when he homered in two straight games at Yankee Stadium in New York

Seattle's Ken Griffey, Jr., tied a record when he blasted home runs in eight straight games.   *Wide World*

as Mattingly looked on. During the streak Mattingly, who was a teammate of Ken Griffey, Sr., said of Junior, "It's kind of cool. It doesn't bother me at all. I hope he breaks it."

Most consecutive games hitting a home run: 8, Ken Griffey, Jr., Seattle (AL), July 20–28, 1995 [Ties Don Mattingly, New York (AL), July 8–18, 1987, and Dale Long, Pittsburgh (NL), May 19–29, 1956]

No Messing with Mesa

CLEVELAND, Ohio, Aug. 20, 1995—With Cleveland setting its sights on its first pennant in more than 40 years, Indian reliever Jose Mesa pitched a scoreless ninth inning today to record his 37th save in 37 attempts for an 8–5 decision over the Milwaukee Brewers at Jacobs Field.

Mesa, who had only two saves to his credit prior to the start of the season, has not given up an earned run since June 8 and sports a 1.12 earned-run average.

The 37 consecutive saves without a blown opportunity breaks Dennis Eckersley's single-season mark of 36 set in 1992 with Oakland. The major league record of 41 over three seasons (1993–95), was set by San Francisco's Rod Beck.

The victory raised Cleveland's league-leading record to 71–34 and gave the Indians a 19-game lead over second-place Milwaukee in the AL's Central Division.

Most saves without a blown attempt, one season: 37, Jose Mesa, Cleveland (AL), 1995

New Iron Horse

DETROIT, Mich., Oct. 1, 1995—Cal Ripkin, Jr., ended the season today on a quiet note, going 0-for-2 with two walks as the Orioles beat the Detroit Tigers, 4–0, in a game that had no bearing on the pennant race.

Though he extended his own record by playing in his 2,153rd straight game, the scene was a far cry from the tumultuous atmosphere at Baltimore's Camden Yards on Sept. 6 when Ripken broke the one baseball record many said would never be broken: Lou Gehrig's 2,130 consecutive games played.

The 35-year-old Ripken had played in every game for the 13-plus seasons when he stepped on the field against the California Angels that September night before a packed house of 46,272 and millions more watching on national television and around the world.

The scoreboard says it for Baltimore's Cal Ripken, Jr., when he broke Lou Gehrig's consecutive-game record in 1995. *Wide World*

Among the spectators on hand was Joe DiMaggio, a Yankee teammate of Gehrig when he took himself out of the lineup May 2, 1939—never to play again. That broke Gehrig's string of 2,130 straight games played, beginning June 1, 1925.

Ripken, playing in the record-smashing 2,131st game, swatted his 15th homer of the season in the home half of the fourth inning. That brought a nice round of applause, but nothing like the ovation at the end of the next half-inning, when the game became official with Baltimore ahead, 3–1, en route to a 4–2 victory over the Angels.

With the crowd on its feet applauding and cheering and the numbers 2–1–3–1 appearing 10-feet high on the scoreboard, Ripken circled the field, shaking hands, and receiving pats on the back from box-seat VIPs and bleacherites alike.

During an hour-long ceremony at the end of the game, Ripken voiced what the moment meant to him: "Tonight I stand here, overwhelmed, as my name is linked with the great and courageous Lou Gehrig. I'm truly humbled to have our names spoken in the same breath."

Most consecutive games played, career: 2,153, Cal Ripken Jr., Baltimore (AL), May 30, 1982–Oct. 1, 1995

A Mariner's Haul

SEATTLE, Wash., Oct. 8, 1995—Seattle's Edgar Martinez broke a 6–6 tie with a grand-slam homer in the bottom of the eighth inning today to lead the Mariners to an 11–8 victory over the New York Yankees and tie their opening round of the American League playoff series at two games apiece.

The 32-year-old Martinez, who won his second regular-season batting title this year, had earlier smashed a three-run homer to give him seven runs batted in, a single-game record for postseason play.

Martinez has been a thorn in the Yankees' side all season long, getting 18 hits in 46 at-bats for a .391 average while slamming seven home runs and driving in 20 runs. In the first four games of the playoffs, Martinez is batting .600 against the Yankees and has a pair of homers and 10 RBIs.

Most runs batted in, postseason game: 7, Edgar Martinez, Seattle (AL), vs. New York, Oct. 8, 1995

PRO FOOTBALL

Nevers-Nevers Land

CHICAGO, Ill., Nov. 28, 1929—The holiday air permeated snow-covered Comiskey Park today as a Thanksgiving Day crowd of 8,000 watched the Bears and Cardinals battle for the championship of Chicago. Earlier, the two teams had played to a scoreless tie, and with losing records neither was headed for a championship of anything but the Windy City.

An injured Red Grange said he was ready to play for the Bears, and an overweight, overage Jim Thorpe came out of retirement again to put in a token appearance with the Cardinals and add to the festivities. Thorpe wasn't going to be much help to the South Siders, but the Cards were counting on powerful Ernie Nevers, the product of Superior, Wis., who went to Stanford and almost single-handedly took on Notre Dame's Four Horsemen in the 1925 Rose Bowl.

Nevers scored the second time the Cards had the ball, going 20 yards in the swirling snow behind a block by Duke Slater. Before the first half was over, Nevers scored twice more and booted a pair of extra points to give the Cardinals a 20–0 halftime lead.

The second half was almost a carbon copy of the first, with Nevers scoring three more touchdowns and kicking two points after. The Bears tallied on a 60-yard pass from Walt Homer to Garland Grange, Red's brother. Nevers' six touchdowns established an NFL record, as did his total of 40 points.

Most points scored, game: 40, Ernie Nevers, Chicago Cardinals, vs. Chicago Bears, Nov. 28, 1929 (6 touchdowns, 4 PATs)

Groundless Fears

LOS ANGELES, Cal., Dec. 3, 1950—Led by the pass-catching of Tom Fears, the Los Angeles Rams went on a record-setting binge today in beating the Green Bay Packers, 51–14, to clinch at least a tie for the championship of the NFL's National Conference.

As the Rams were establishing seasonal records in 10 team offensive categories, the 6-foot 2-inch, 215-pound Fears was catching a record 18 passes to establish a single-game mark. The old league record of 14 receptions was set in 1940 by Don Looney of Philadelphia, and tied by Green Bay's Don Hutson in 1942, the Chicago Bears' Jimmy Keane in 1949, and the New York Bulldogs' Ralph Heywood in 1949.

With Norm Van Brocklin and Bob Waterfield passing, receivers like Fears and Elroy Hirsch, and runners like Glenn Davis and Tank Younger, the Rams have been an explosive offensive team all season. Just two weeks ago, against the New York Yanks, the Rams gained 636 yards, while the Yanks were picking up 497 yards to establish a record for most yards gained by two teams in one game: 1,133.

Most receptions, game: 18, Tom Fears, Los Angeles Rams, vs. Green Bay Packers, Dec. 3, 1950
Most yards gained, both teams, game: 1,133, Los Angeles Rams (636) and New York Yanks (497), Nov. 19, 1950

The Flingin' Dutchman

LOS ANGELES, Cal., Sept. 28, 1951—Young Norm Van Brocklin made Ram fans forget about the injured Bob Waterfield and Glenn Davis tonight as he passed for 554 yards in leading Los Angeles past the New York Yanks, 54–14.

Van Brocklin, who played college ball at Oregon, bettered the efforts of Chicago Bear quarterback Johnny Lujack, who passed for 468 yards two years ago.

The Los Angeles Rams' Norm Van Brocklin passed for 544 yards against the New York Yanks in 1951. *UPI*

Playing before a crowd of 30,315, Van Brocklin threw five touchdown aerials, four of them to Elroy "Crazylegs" Hirsch. The Rams' 34 first downs and 735 total yards also established league marks.

Most yardage, passing, game: 554, Norm Van Brocklin, Los Angeles Rams, vs. New York Yanks, Sept. 28, 1951
Most yards gained, game, one team: 735, Los Angeles Rams, vs. New York Yanks, Sept. 28, 1951

On the Right Track

LOS ANGELES, Cal., Dec. 14, 1952—Dick "Night Train" Lane put the Los Angeles Rams into a playoff with the Detroit Lions, but he won't be there to enjoy the fruits of his labor.

Lane intercepted three passes and ran back one for a touchdown today to spark the defending champion

Rams to their eighth straight victory, a 28–14 decision over Pittsburgh. The three interceptions gave Lane a record total of 14 for the season, surpassing the mark of 12 shared by Don Sandifer of Washington and Spec Sanders of the old New York Yankees.

A crowd of more than 70,000 was on hand to see Norm Van Brocklin throw a touchdown pass to Elroy Hirsch and two to Tom Fears as Bob Waterfield, in his last game for the Rams, was relegated to kicking extra points.

Pittsburgh quarterback Jim Finks was victimized four times by the Ram defense, and it was the last interception that brought Lane the record and put him out of the playoff game. Lane, a product of Scottsbluff (Neb.) Junior College, was brought down hard after the interception, wrenching his knee and severely spraining his ankle.

Most interceptions, season: 14, Dick "Night Train" Lane, Los Angeles Rams, 1952

Dick "Night Train" Lane of the Los Angeles Rams holds the record with 14 interceptions in a season.   *UPI*

Green Bay's Paul Hornung scores against Los Angeles in the final game of his 176-point season. *UPI*

Golden Boy

LOS ANGELES, Cal., Dec. 17, 1960—Paul Hornung scored a fourth-quarter touchdown and followed that with his fifth extra point of the day to lead the Green Bay Packers past the Los Angeles Rams, 35–21, and on to their first divisional championship in 16 years.

Hornung, called "the Golden Boy" because of his golden locks and ability to come up with the "money play," scored on a one-yard plunge. The score, and extra points, brought his season's point total to a record 176. Hornung, who won the Heisman Trophy four years ago as a quarterback at Notre Dame, had broken the old scoring record of 138 points two weeks ago when he scored 23 points against the Chicago Bears. The record that Hornung broke had been set by Don Hutson in 1942. Hutson, incidentally, was on that last Packer team to win a divisional title, in 1944.

Most points, season: 176, Paul Hornung, Green Bay Packers, 1960 (15 touchdowns, 41 PATs, 15 field goals)

Running Wild

CHICAGO, Ill., Dec. 12, 1965—With the NFL's Western Division championship at stake, Chicago's Gale Sayers went on a scoring binge today in tying a 36-year-old record with a six-touchdown performance against the San Francisco 49ers. Winning 61–20, kept the Bears in contention with the Baltimore Colts and Green Bay Packers. (In Baltimore, Green Bay's Paul Hornung scored five TDs in a 42–27 Packer triumph.)

The 6-foot, 200-pound Sayers, a rookie out of Kansas University, opened the scoring after gathering in a screen pass from Rudy Bukich. The play covered 80 yards, all of it on Sayers' running. The soft-spoken halfback then scored on runs of 21, 7, 50, and 1 yard before returning a punt 85 yards for his sixth touchdown, matching the number scored by Ernie Nevers of the Chicago Cardinals against the Bears on Thanksgiving Day, 1929, and Dub Jones of Cleveland, also against the Bears, in 1951.

Gale Sayers of the Chicago Bears heads toward one of his six touchdowns against the San Francisco 49ers in 1965. *UPI*

After the game, Sayers was awarded the game ball and thus became the first player in Bear history to be awarded two game balls in one season. In addition to his TDs, Sayers picked up 113 yards rushing, 89 yards on pass receptions, and 134 yards on punt returns.

On no count was it a great day for the 49ers, especially for placekicker Tommy Davis. He missed an extra-point attempt. It was the first extra point he failed to convert since he began playing in the NFL in 1959. The onetime Louisiana State star had kicked a record 234 points in a row.

Most touchdowns, game: 6, Gale Sayers, Chicago Bears, vs. San Francisco 49ers, Dec. 12, 1965 (Ties Ernie Nevers, Chicago Cardinals, vs. Chicago Bears, Nov. 28, 1929; William "Dub" Jones, Cleveland Browns, vs. Chicago Bears, Nov. 25, 1951)
Most consecutive extra points: 234, Tommy Davis, San Francisco 49ers, Sept. 27, 1959, to Dec. 5, 1965

Doing It Up Brown

ST. LOUIS, Mo., Dec. 21, 1965—The Cleveland Browns' Jim Brown, as stormy in temperament as he is talented in football, saw most of his last regular-season game from the bench today. Big No. 32 was ejected from the game in the first half after fighting with the St. Louis Cardinals' Joe Robb.

Before he left the game, though, the 6-foot 3-inch, 230-pound Brown gained 74 yards on 11 carries, scored his 21st touchdown of the season, the 126th of his career. His touchdown contributed to Cleveland's 27–24 victory over St. Louis that gave the Browns the best record in the NFL with 11 wins and 3 losses.

Earlier in the season, Brown became the first player to rush for 100 touchdowns in a career. Among the records of Brown, who never missed a game in his nine-year career, are:

Most seasons leading the league, rushing touchdowns: 5, Jim Brown, Cleveland Browns, 1957–59, 1963, 1965

Highest rushing average, career: 5.22 yards per carry, Jim Brown, Cleveland Browns, 1957–65
Most seasons leading the league, rushing: 8, Jim Brown, Cleveland Browns, 1957–61, 1963–65

The Cleveland Browns' Jimmy Brown scores the last touchdown of his career against the St. Louis Cardinals.   *UPI*

Just for Kicks

PITTSBURGH, Pa., Sept. 24, 1967—Jim Bakken has nothing to kick about now. The former reserve quarterback from the University of Wisconsin and full-time kicking specialist for the St. Louis Cardinals booted an unprecedented seven field goals today as St. Louis beat Pittsburgh, 28–14.

In addition to making kicks of 18, 24, 33, 29, 24, 32, and 23 yards, Bakken missed two attempts, from 45 and 50 yards away. The nine attempts are an NFL record.

Bakken's harvest surpassed the six field goals registered last season by Garo Yepremian of the Detroit Lions against the Minnesota Vikings.

The contribution of the Cardinals' Larry Wilson went largely unnoticed. "Don't I get any credit for holding the ball?" Wilson asked after the game.

Most field goals attempted, game: 9, Jim Bakken, St. Louis Cardinals, vs. Pittsburgh Steelers, Sept. 24, 1967

Kapp-ital Performance

BLOOMINGTON, Minn., Sept. 28, 1969—Most sports fans' minds were on baseball today as the Atlanta Braves clinched the National League's Western Division pennant to join the New York Mets, Minnesota Twins, and Baltimore Orioles in baseball's new-fangled intra-league playoffs that were instituted this season.

But Chicano Joe Kapp and the Minnesota Vikings put on a record-breaking performance that made folks in Metropolitan Stadium here forget about the summer sport. Kapp, the University of California quarterback who played in Canada before becoming a Viking, hit six different receivers with seven touchdown passes, equaling the passing performances of Sid Luckman in 1943, Y. A. Tittle in 1962, George Blanda in 1961, and Adrian Burk in 1954. Burk, who played for the Philadelphia Eagles, was on the field today, working the game as a back judge.

With Vice President Spiro Agnew—former governor of Maryland—in the stands to root for the defending champion Baltimore Colts, Kapp hit Gene Washington twice and Dave Osborn, Bob Grim, Kent Kramer, John Beasley, and Jim Lindsey once each to lead Minnesota past Baltimore, 52–14. Overall, Kapp connected with 12 different receivers in passing for 499 yards before a sell-out crowd of 47,644.

Most touchdown passes thrown, game: 7, Joe Kapp, Minnesota Vikings, vs. Baltimore Colts, Sept. 28, 1969 (Ties Sid Luckman, Chicago Bears, vs. New York Giants, Nov. 14, 1943; Adrian Burk, Philadelphia Eagles, vs. Washington Redskins, Oct. 17, 1954; George Blanda, Houston Oilers, vs. New York Titans, Nov. 19, 1961; Y. A. Tittle, New York Giants, vs. Washington Redskins, Oct. 28, 1962)

Minnesota's Joe Kapp passed for six touchdowns against Baltimore in 1969.
Malcolm Emmons

The Longest Field Goal

NEW ORLEANS, La., Nov. 8, 1970—Trailing 17–16 with two seconds left to play and the ball on their own 45-yard line, New Orleans Saints' coach J.D. Roberts sent in kicking specialist Tom Dempsey to try a field goal against the Detroit Lions. The 6-foot 1-inch, 265-pound Dempsey set up 10 yards behind the line of scrimmage, with holder Joe Scarpati kneeling at the Lion 37. Jackie Burkett snapped the ball, Scarpati set it down, and Dempsey kicked.

The final gun sounded just before the cheers erupted from the 66,910 fans in Tulane's Sugar Bowl Stadium as the ball sailed through the uprights. The 63-yard kick was the longest field goal ever made in an NFL game, surpassing the old record of 56 yards by Baltimore's Bert Rechichar against the Chicago Bears in 1953.

Dempsey, who was born without a right hand and with a clubbed right foot, the one he kicks with, said afterward he couldn't even see the goal posts. But he

This is the special shoe Tom Dempsey of the New Orleans Saints wore for his record field goal against the Detroit Lions in 1970. *UPI*

didn't have to see that far. "I saw the referee's hands go up and everybody started yelling and I knew it was good," Dempsey recounted happily.

Longest field goal: 63 yards, Tom Dempsey, New Orleans Saints, vs. Detroit Lions, Nov. 8, 1970

Jack Be Nimble, Jack Be Quick

GREEN BAY, Wis., Sept. 24, 1972—The oldest record in the books was erased today by quick and alert Jack Tatum and a misjudgment by the officials.

Tatum, playing safety for the Oakland Raiders, scooped up a bouncing football in one end zone and raced 104 yards down the sideline to the other end of the field for a touchdown that provided the margin of victory in Oakland's 20–14 victory over the Green Bay Packers. The officials ruled that the loose ball had been fumbled by MacArthur Lane and could legally be advanced. Videotape replay later showed, however, that Lane had bobbled a pitchout and never had control of the ball. In that case, Tatum should not have been able to advance it.

But it was ruled a fumble, and so Tatum's name replaces that of George Halas of the Chicago Bears, who picked up a fumble and traveled 98 yards for a touchdown against the Oorang Indians in an NFL game on Nov. 4, 1923.

Longest return of a recovered opponent's fumble: 104 yards, Jack Tatum, Oakland Raiders, vs. Green Bay Packers, Sept. 24, 1972

O.J. on the Rush

MIAMI, Fla., Dec. 5, 1976—The Buffalo Bills' O. J. Simpson turned in his longest run of the season—a 75-yard touchdown jaunt in the first quarter—en route to a 203-yard rushing performance that went for naught as the Bills fell to the Miami Dolphins, 45–27, in the Orange Bowl today.

The 75-yard TD, the first score of the day, came as

Always in a hurry, O. J. Simpson was a world-class sprinter who turned on the juice as a ball carrier in football, including the most 200-yard NFL games. *Buffalo Bills/SPS*

part of a 111-yard first-half effort for Simpson, the All-American out of the University of Southern California now in his fifth NFL season. It was a record sixth time in his career that the 6-foot 1-inch, 210-pound Simpson had topped the 200-yard rushing mark.

With Freddie Solomon catching five passes for 114 yards and three touchdowns, Miami improved its record to 6–7, while Buffalo dropped to 2–11.

Most games, 200 or more yards rushing, career: 6, O.J. Simpson, Buffalo Bills, 1969–77

The Scrambler's Legacy

LOS ANGELES, Cal., Dec. 31, 1978—Quarterback Fran Tarkenton had made it to three Super Bowls with the Minnesota Vikings, but the Los Angeles Rams derailed the Vikings today, 34–10, in the NFC divisional playoffs.

It was Tarkenton's last game in a celebrated 18-year career that began in 1961 with the infant Vikings, when

Nobody played more games at quarterback than Fran Tarkenton. *UPI*

he was a third-round draft choice out of Georgia. Traded to the New York Giants in 1967, he came back to the Vikings in 1972, and now it's all over.

"The Scrambler" went out on top even if he never won a Super Bowl. He started his first game and he started his last one. He played in more games than any other quarterback in NFL history (257). And he hung up his cleats today with career marks for most passes completed (3,686), most passes attempted (6,467), most yards gained passing (47,003), and most touchdown passes (342).

Most games at quarterback: 257, Fran Tarkenton, Minnesota Vikings, 1961–66, 1972–78; New York Giants, 1967–71

A Touch of Green

IRVING, Tex., Oct. 21, 1979—Roy Green of the St. Louis Cardinals, a rookie safety out of Henderson State, was six yards in his own end zone today when he took a Dallas kickoff.

He was touched only once—by an off-balance arm swipe by Doug Cosbie on the Cardinal 40—as he sped to a touchdown and into the record book. His 106-yard romp tied the mark shared by Al Carmichael of the Green Bay Packers and Noland Smith of the Kansas City Chiefs.

It was the Cardinals' only touchdown as Dallas prevailed, 22–13. Green said, "I guess someday the record will be broken . . . maybe by me."

Longest return of a kickoff: 106 yards, Roy Green, St. Louis Cardinals, vs. Dallas Cowboys, Oct. 21, 1979 (Ties Noland Smith, Kansas City Chiefs, vs. Denver Broncos, Dec. 17, 1967; Al Carmichael, Green Bay Packers, vs. Chicago Bears, Oct. 7, 1956)

Roy Green of the St. Louis Cardinals sped 106 yards on a kickoff return in 1979.   *St. Louis Cardinals/SPS*

A Viking's Voyage

FOXBORO, Mass., Dec. 15, 1979—For 41-year-old Jim Marshall it was farewell today. The 6-foot 4-inch, 240-pound defensive end of the Minnesota Vikings played the final game of a 20-year career.

It was tarnished only slightly by the fact that the New England Patriots beat the Vikings, 27–23, but Marshall's lifetime marks will be remembered more than the score of the game.

A Kentuckian who played for Ohio State before breaking in with the Cleveland Browns in 1960, Marshall joined the Vikings in their first year in 1961 and played in every game since then.

His 282 consecutive games are an NFL record. So are his 19 seasons with one club and his 29 opponents' fumbles recovered.

Most consecutive games played, career: 282, Jim Marshall, Cleveland Browns, 1960; Minnesota Vikings, 1961–79

Most seasons, one club: 19, Jim Marshall, Minnesota Vikings,
*   1961–79*
Most opponents' fumbles recovered: 29, Jim Marshall, Cleveland
*   Browns, 1960; Minnesota Vikings, 1961–79*

Dorsett's Dash

MINNEAPOLIS, Minn., Jan. 3, 1983—The Minnesota
Vikings were leading the Dallas Cowboys, 24–13, in

Dallas' Tony Dorsett got off a 99-yard touchdown run against
Minnesota in 1983.   *Dallas Cowboys/SPS*

the final quarter tonight, and Dallas was on its own one-yard line following Timmy Newsome's fumble of a kickoff.

A noisy home crowd of 60,000 in the Metrodome suddenly came to its feet when Tony Dorsett burst up the middle on first down, broke to the outside, and shot up the right sideline. At the 30, he brushed off a tackle attempt by Willie Teal and went on to an NFL-record 99-yard run.

Dorsett's gallop was to no avail, however, as the Vikings wound up winning the game, 31–27.

The longest run from scrimmage had been 97 yards by Bob Gage of the Pittsburgh Steelers against the Chicago Bears on Dec. 4, 1949, and Andy Uram of the Green Bay Packers against the Chicago Cardinals on Oct. 8, 1939.

Longest run from scrimmage: 99 yards, Tony Dorsett, Dallas Cowboys, vs. Minnesota Vikings, Jan. 3, 1983 (TD)

Eric the Ram

SAN FRANCISCO, Cal., Dec. 14, 1984—Eric Dickerson, who has rushed for more yardage in one NFL season than any other running back, was held to 98 yards tonight as the Los Angeles Rams failed to clinch a playoff berth in a 19–16 loss to the San Francisco 49ers, in the season's final regular-season game for both teams.

Playing before a national television audience in an unusual Thursday night game, Joe Montana hit eight straight passes—two for touchdowns—in the first quarter to lead the 49ers, who became the first team in NFL history to win 15 games in a season as they finished 15–1.

The Rams, whose record dropped to 10–6, must wait until this weekend's games involving the New York Giants, Washington Redskins, St. Louis Cardinals, and Dallas Cowboys before finding out if they qualify for a wild-card playoff berth.

The Los Angeles Rams' Eric Dickerson rushed for the most yards in a season in 1984.
Vic Milton

The 6-foot 3-inch, 218-pound Dickerson broke the single-season rushing mark last Sunday, gaining 215 yards on 27 carries against Houston in a 27–16 Ram victory.

Tonight was a different story for the former Southern Methodist star, however, as he gained just 19 yards on seven carries in the first quarter before fumbling in the second, which set up a Ray Wersching field goal.

Dickerson redeemed himself somewhat, picking up 76 yards and a touchdown in the period. In the third quarter, he carried four times and showed a net gain of only one yard. He left the game early in the fourth period and sat out the rest of the way. On the season, Dickerson has gained 2,105 yards. The former mark of 2,003 yards was set by Buffalo's O.J. Simpson during a 14-game season in 1973.

Most yards rushing, season: 2,105, Eric Dickerson, Los Angeles Rams, 1984

Splash of the Dolphins

MIAMI, Fla., Dec. 17, 1984—A winning combination all season long, Miami Dolphin quarterback Dan Marino and wide receiver Mark Clayton clicked tonight for a touchdown in the final minute of play to knock the Dallas Cowboys out of the NFL playoffs, 28–21.

It was Clayton's third touchdown reception of the game, giving him 18 for the season, an NFL mark, and it also enabled Marino to finish the year with 48 touchdown passes, 362 completions, and 5,084 yards passing.

Clayton's 18 erased the old mark of 17 jointly held by Don Hutson of the Green Bay Packers, Elroy Hirsch of the Los Angeles Rams, and Bill Groman of the Houston Oilers.

Earlier in the season Marino had surpassed the record 36 touchdown passes held by Houston's George Blanda and Y. A. Tittle of the New York Giants.

Most touchdown passes, season: 48, Dan Marino, Miami Dolphins, 1984

Norwegian Boots

MINNEAPOLIS, Minn., Dec. 22, 1985—A storybook finish called for Jan Stenerud to kick the winning field goal for the Minnesota Vikings today against the Philadelphia Eagles. But the Vikings lost, 37–35, when time ran out as they moved into position for one last 33-yard field-goal attempt.

And so the 43-year-old Norwegian-born Stenerud went into retirement with a record total of 373 field goals over the course of a 19-year career with the Kansas City Chiefs, Green Bay Packers, and the Vikings.

Most field goals, career: 373, Jan Stenerud, Kansas City Chiefs, 1967–79; Green Bay Packers, 1980–83; Minnesota Vikings, 1984–85

An Aerial Streak

GREEN BAY, Wis., Dec. 6, 1987—Completing his first 17 passes for a record 22 in a row today, the San Francisco 49ers' Joe Montana blitzed the Green Bay Packers, 23–12.

Last week the unerring quarterback had connected with his last five aerials against the Cleveland Browns, setting the stage for the new mark that eclipsed the 20 straight completions by the Cincinnati Bengals' Ken Anderson against the Houston Oilers on Jan. 2, 1983.

Two of Montana's passes went for touchdowns today, one a 57-yarder to Jerry Rice that iced the game with 7:32 remaining. It was the 49ers' 10th victory in 12 games.

Most consecutive passes completed: 22, Joe Montana, San Francisco 49ers, vs. Cleveland Browns (5), Nov. 29, 1987; San Francisco 49ers, vs. Green Bay Packers (17), Dec. 6, 1987.

Sweetness Rushes Out

LOS ANGELES, Cal., Dec. 27, 1987—Walter Payton, the man they call Sweetness because of his smooth running style, closed out his career with the Bears by gaining 82 yards on 20 carries as he led Chicago to a 6–3 victory today over the Los Angeles Raiders in the Coliseum.

Chicago's Walter Payton charged his way into the record book during a 13-year career.   *Vic Milton*

The game almost ended on a sour note for Payton, who fumbled on his last carry with 1:31 left to play. Bill Pickel of the Raiders recovered on the 50, but Los Angeles turned the ball over on downs without getting close enough to try a field goal.

The 80 yards rushing gave Payton a total of 16,726 yards for his 13-year career, 4,414 more than Jimmy Brown, who set the record playing with the Cleveland Browns from 1957 through 1967.

Payton, who spent his whole pro career with the Bears after coming out of Jackson State in 1975, also holds a number of other records, including the single-game rushing mark of 275 yards set against the Minnesota Vikings on Nov. 20, 1977.

Most yards rushing, career: 16,726, Walter Payton, Chicago Bears, 1975–87

Most rushing attempts, career: 3,838, Walter Payton, Chicago Bears, 1975–87

Most seasons 1,000 yards or more rushing: 10, Walter Payton, Chicago Bears, 1976–81, 1983–86

Most games 100 or more yards rushing, career: 77, Walter Payton, Chicago Bears, 1975–87

Most touchdowns rushing, career: 110, Walter Payton, Chicago Bears, 1975–87

Most yards gained rushing, game: 275, Walter Payton, Chicago Bears, vs. Minnesota Vikings, Nov. 20, 1977

Rice in the End Zone

SAN FRANCISCO, Cal., Dec. 27, 1987—Capping a record-smashing season, Jerry Rice hauled in two touchdown passes from Steve Young today as the San Francisco 49ers routed the Los Angeles Rams, 48–0, and clinched the NFC West title.

The 6-foot 2-inch Rice, a third-year player out of Mississippi Valley State, caught three passes, including a 22-yard scoring strike in the first quarter and a 50-yard TD bomb in the second to give him a record 22 touchdowns for the season. This marked the 13th straight game (another record) in which Rice has caught at least one scoring pass.

Last week against Atlanta, Rice broke the old TD reception mark of 18 set by Miami's Mark Clayton in 1984, as well as the consecutive-game mark of 11 set by Elroy Hirsch of the Los Angeles Rams in 1950–51 and equaled by Pittsburgh's Buddy Dial in the 1959 and '60 seasons.

Most touchdowns on pass receptions, season: 22, Jerry Rice, San Francisco 49ers, 1987

Most consecutive games with a touchdown reception: 13, Jerry Rice, San Francisco 49ers, 1986–87

San Francisco's Jerry Rice caught the most touchdowns in a season in 1987.   *San Francisco 49ers/SPS*

Feat of Foot

MINNEAPOLIS, Minn., Nov. 5, 1989—The Minnesota Vikings couldn't score a touchdown today, but fortunately for them, Rich Karlis kicked field goals and Mike Merriweather played defense, so that the team beat the Los Angeles Rams, 23–21, in overtime at the Metrodome.

Two minutes into the overtime, the Rams were stopped on their first series and forced to punt. Merriweather, the former Pittsburgh Steeler, blocked Dale Hatcher's punt at the 12-yard line. The ball rolled out of the end zone for a safety, giving Minnesota a two-point victory in the first overtime game to be decided by a safety.

The Vikings were fortunate to be in overtime. Unable to put the ball in the end zone all day long, it took a 40-yard Karlis field goal with eight seconds left in regulation time to send the game into overtime.

The 6-foot, 180-pound Karlis, picked up on waivers earlier this season after spending all of his career with Denver, was the entire scoring offense for the Vikes. He gave Minnesota the early lead with a 20-yard field goal in the first quarter, then made kicks of 24, 22, and 25 yards to give the home team a 12–7 lead at half.

Field goals of 29 and 36 yards in the third quarter set up Karlis' tying effort. That came after the Rams tallied two TDs in the final quarter.

The seven field goals by Karlis, who played collegiately at the University of Cincinnati, tied the NFL single-game record set by Jim Bakken of the St. Louis Cardinals.

Most field goals, game: 7, Rich Karlis, Minnesota Vikings, vs. Los Angeles Rams, Nov. 5, 1989 (Ties Jim Bakken, St. Louis Cardinals, vs. Pittsburgh Steelers, Sept. 24, 1967)

Flipping to Flipper

NEW ORLEANS, La., Nov. 26, 1989—With Willie "Flipper" Anderson putting on a record-setting performance, the Los Angeles Rams stormed from behind with 17 points to beat New Orleans, 20–17, in a nationally televised game at the Superdome tonight.

Going into the fourth quarter, the Rams were trailing, 17–3, and Anderson had gained 141 yards on six receptions. With Jim Everett on the throwing end, the 6-foot, 170-pound Anderson gathered in three more passes for 76 yards to set up a 5-yard TD run by Buford McGee. Less than two minutes later, with just 62 seconds left in regulation time, Anderson gathered in a 15-yard scoring strike to knot the game at 17–17.

Anderson, a high school quarterback in Paulsboro, N.J., before switching to receiver at UCLA, caught two passes in overtime for 40 yards, including a 26-yard effort that set up Mike Lansford's game-winning 31-yard field goal.

Anderson, nicknamed by his grandmother, who thought he made noises like Flipper the dolphin, ended the game with 15 catches for a record 336 yards. The old mark of 309 yards was set by Kansas City's Stephone Paige against San Diego on Dec. 22, 1985.

Most pass reception yardage, game: 336 yards, Willie "Flipper" Anderson, Los Angeles Rams, vs. New Orleans Saints, Nov. 26, 1989

King of the Super Bowl

NEW ORLEANS, La., Jan. 28, 1990—Joe Montana completed 22 of 29 passes for 297 yards and 5 touchdowns as he led the San Francisco 49ers to a 55–10 rout of Denver in winning Super Bowl XXIV at the Superdome today.

The 6-foot 1-inch, 195-pound Montana, who sat out the last 11 minutes of the game, earned his third Super Bowl Most Valuable Player award. This was the 49ers' fourth appearance in the big event in nine years, all winning efforts directed by Montana.

In setting a raft of game and career records, the former Notre Dame quarterback was not intercepted and not really sacked, though he scrambled once for no

San Francisco's Joe Montana won his third Super Bowl MVP award and added to his record collection against Denver in XXIV.   *Wide World*

gain and this is technically scored a sack. After the game, Montana said, "I had excellent protection. My job was easy. I could stay back and look around."

Super Bowl
Most MVP awards: 3, Joe Montana, San Francisco 49ers, XVI, XIX, XXIV
Most consecutive completions, game: 13, Joe Montana, San Francisco 49ers vs. Denver Broncos, 1990
Most touchdown passes, career: 11, Joe Montana, San Francisco 49ers, 4 games
Most yards gained passing, career: 1,142, Joe Montana, San Francisco 49ers, 4 games
Most passes completed, career: 83, Joe Montana, San Francisco 49ers, 4 games
Highest completion percentage, career (minimum 50 attempts): 68.0%, Joe Montana, San Francisco 49ers, 4 games
Fewest interceptions, career (minimum 50 attempts): Joe Montana, San Francisco 49ers, 4 games (no interceptions in 122 attempts)

The Niner Connection

ATLANTA, Ga., Oct. 14, 1990—"It was the best passing game since I became head coach," said George Seifert today after the San Francisco 49ers scored a 45–35 victory over the Atlanta Falcons.

The awesome battery of Joe Montana and Jerry Rice went on a binge—Montana throwing for 476 yards and six touchdowns (five to Rice) as the defending Super Bowl champions extended their league·record for consecutive regular-season victories on the road to 13.

Montana and Rice posted all sorts of team marks, but it was Rice who made an entry in the NFL record book when his five TDs tied the receiving mark shared by Bob Shaw of the Chicago Cardinals and Kellen Winslow of the San Diego Chargers.

Most touchdowns on pass receptions, game: 5, Jerry Rice, San Francisco 49ers, vs. Atlanta Falcons, Oct. 14, 1990 (Ties Bob Shaw, Chicago Cardinals, vs. Baltimore Colts, Oct. 2, 1950, and Kellen Winslow, San Diego Chargers, vs. Oakland Raiders, Nov. 22, 1981)

Sack Time

KANSAS CITY, Mo., Nov. 11, 1990—The Kansas City Chiefs' Derrick Thomas set a record today with seven quarterback sacks, but the eighth one got away. And that hurt.

As time ran out, the Seattle Seahawks' Dave Krieg wiggled loose of the 6-foot 3-inch, 242-pound linebacker and threw a desperation 25-yard touchdown pass to Paul Skansi. Norm Johnson booted the extra point for the Seahawks' 17–16 victory.

Thomas' seven sacks eclipsed Fred Dean's six for the San Francisco 49ers against the New Orleans Saints on Nov. 13, 1983.

Most sacks, game: 7, Derrick Thomas, Kansas City Chiefs, vs. Seattle Seahawks, Nov. 11, 1990

All in a day's work were the seven sacks of Kansas City's Derrick Thomas against Seattle in 1990.   *Wide World*

Pete's Kick

MIAMI, Fla., Jan. 5, 1991—It was a tale of two kickers—the Miami Dolphins' Pete Stoyanovich and the Kansas City Chiefs' Nick Lowery.

It came down to the final seconds, Dolphins leading 17–16 with the winning team to reach the AFC semifinals. Lowery had made 24 consecutive field goals, three in this game already. But his 52-yard attempt fell inches short. It was on to Buffalo for Miami.

Stoyanovich, a second-year performer out of Indiana, expressed sympathy for Lowery, but he had the last laugh. The young Dolphin had kicked a playoff-record 58-yarder in the second quarter. It broke the 54-yard mark that had been held by the Detroit Lions' Ed Murray (vs. San Francisco, 1983).

Longest field goal, playoffs: 58 yards, Pete Stoyanovich, Miami Dolphins, vs. Kansas City Chiefs, Jan. 5, 1991

Thou Shalt Not Intercept!

CLEVELAND, Ohio, Nov. 10, 1991—Bernie Kosar surpassed a 16-year-old record today that had been set by Bart Starr of the Green Bay Packers.

Displaying his pinpoint accuracy, the Cleveland

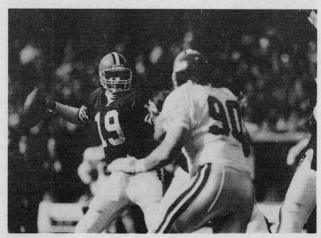

Cleveland's Bernie Kosar streaked past Green Bay's Bart Starr for a no-interceptions mark in 1990.   *Wide World*

Browns' quarterback extended his streak to 308 passes without an interception. It came to an end when corner-back Ben Smith of the Philadelphia Eagles speared a Kosar pass in the second quarter. Starr had held the record at 294 since 1965.

But it wasn't all celebration for Kosar, whose three touchdown passes gave the Browns a 30–17 first-half lead. Quarterback Jim McMahon led a comeback that resulted in a 32–30 Philadelphia victory.

Most consecutive passes without interception: 308, Bernie Kosar, Cleveland Browns, 1990–91

His First Touchdown

ORCHARD PARK, N.Y., October 4, 1992—Louis Oliver had never scored a touchdown—not in high school, not at the U. of Florida, not in three years as a pro safety with the Miami Dolphins.

But today he got on the board with a bang. The 6-foot 2-inch, 224-pounder ran for a record-tying 103-yard touchdown on an intercepted pass as the Dolphins walloped the Buffalo Bills, 37–10.

Oliver's sprint came on a Jim Kelly pass intended for Thurman Thomas and was the longest since the San Diego Chargers' Vencie Glenn set the mark against the Denver Broncos on November 29, 1987.

Longest return of an interception: 103, Louis Oliver, Miami Dolphins, vs. Buffalo Bills, Oct. 4, 1992 (Ties Vencie Glenn, San Diego Chargers, vs. Denver Broncos, Nov. 29, 1987)

Vinny, Vidi, Vici

LOS ANGELES, Cal., Dec. 26, 1993—It was a day-late Christmas present for the Cleveland Browns' Vinny Testaverde. But it wasn't something willingly given today by the Los Angeles Rams.

"It was so simple," grumbled Rams safety Anthony Newman. "It was just throw and catch."

He was referring to Testaverde's sharp-shooting—21 of 23 passes for a one-game record of 91.3 percent. It led to a 42–14 rout of the Rams.

The old mark was 90.9 (21–19), set by the Cincinnati Bengals' Ken Anderson against the Pittsburgh Steelers on Nov. 10, 1974.

Highest completion percentage, game: 91.3, Vinny Testaverde, Cleveland Browns, vs. Los Angeles Rams, Dec. 26, 1993

The Right Connection

LOS ANGELES, Cal., Dec. 31, 1993—A couple of Jeffs collaborated today to land the Los Angeles Raiders in the playoffs.

Playing against the Denver Broncos, quarterback Jeff Hostetler passed for three touchdowns, including one that tied the score at 30–all as time ran out. In overtime, Hostetler drove the Raiders 49 yards to set up Jeff Jaeger, who had already kicked three field goals.

Jaeger connected for the game-winner. More than that, he wound up with a record-tying 35 field goals for the season.

Most field goals, season: 35, Jeff Jaeger, Los Angeles Raiders, 1993 (Ties Ali Haji-Sheikh, New York Giants, 1983)

Many Happy Returns

NEW ORLEANS, La., Oct. 23, 1994—It was one glorious day for rocket cornerback Tyrone Hughes of the New Orleans Saints. And for the Los Angeles Rams' Robert Bailey as well.

Running wild in a 37–34 victory, Hughes posted 98- and 92-yard touchdowns on kickoff returns and by game's end he had set two records and shared in a third.

The 5-foot 9-inch, 175-pound Hughes totaled 304 yards for a record in kickoff returns, surpassing the 294 garnered by the Detroit Lions' Wally Triplett against the Los Angeles Rams on Oct. 29, 1950. And Hughes' combined kickoff-return and punt-return yardage of 347 erased the record of 294 shared by Triplett (against the Rams on Oct. 29, 1950) and the Rams' Woodley Lewis (against the Lions on Oct. 18, 1953).

Hughes' two scores also tied the mark for most touchdowns on kickoff returns.

Although it was a losing cause for the Rams, corner-back Bailey had a shining moment when he returned a punt 103 yards. He broke the standard shared by four players, most recently by the New York Jets' Terance Mathis against the Dallas Cowboys on Nov. 4, 1990.

Most yards, kickoff returns, game: 304, Tyrone Hughes, New Orleans Saints, vs. Los Angeles Rams, Oct. 23, 1994

Most combined yards, punt and kickoff returns, game: 347, Tyrone Hughes, New Orleans Saints, vs. Los Angeles Rams, Oct. 23, 1994 (p-43, k-304)

Most touchdowns, kickoff returns, game: 2, Tyrone Hughes, New Orleans Saints, vs. Los Angeles Rams, Oct. 23, 1994 (Ties Timmy Brown, Philadelphia Eagles, vs. Dallas Cowboys, Nov. 6, 1966; Travis Williams, Green Bay Packers, vs. Cleveland Browns, Nov. 12, 1967; Ron Brown, Los Angeles Rams, vs. Green Bay Packers, Nov. 24, 1985)

Longest punt return: 103 yards, Robert Bailey, Los Angeles Rams, vs. New Orleans Saints, Oct. 23, 1994

Bombs Unlimited

FOXBORO, Mass., Nov. 13, 1994—Drew Bledsoe staged an aerial circus today as the New England Patriots rallied from a 20–0 deficit to overcome the Minnesota Vikings, 26–20, in overtime.

The former Washington State star, in his third pro season, established NFL marks for attempts (70) and completions (45) in a game. His second-half exploits in a no-huddle offense were marked by three touchdown passes, the winning score coming on a 14-yarder to Kevin Turner.

Bledsoe's attempts record erased the 68 thrown by the Houston Oilers' George Blanda against the Buffalo

Bills on Nov. 1, 1964. The completion mark had been 42, by the New York Jets' Richard Todd, against the San Francisco 49ers on Sept. 21, 1980.

Most pass attempts, game: 70, Drew Bledsoe, New England Patriots, vs. Minnesota Vikings, Nov. 13, 1994 (OT)
Most completions, game: 45, Drew Bledsoe, New England Patriots, vs. Minnesota Vikings, Nov. 13, 1994 (OT)

A Pitcher and a Catcher

MINNEAPOLIS, Minn., Dec. 26, 1994—Playing without injured quarterback Warren Moon, the Minnesota Vikings (10–6) clinched the NFC Central title tonight, defeating the San Francisco 49ers, 21–14.

The 49ers (11–3), already winners of the NFC West, rested Steve Young and Jerry Rice for much of the game, but for the time he was in, Young hit 12 of 13 passes to complete the season with an NFL-record quarterback rating of 112.8 and win his fourth consecutive passing title. He surpassed ex-49er Joe Montana's 112.4 in 1989.

In winning, the Vikings forced four turnovers, including a fumble that rookie cornerback DeWayne Washington returned 17 yards for a touchdown.

Sean Salisbury, Moon's replacement, had trouble finding the Vikings' most potent receivers—Cris Carter and Jake Reed—but Carter caught three to increase his record for pass receptions in a season to 122.

Highest pass rating, season: 112.8, Steve Young, San Francisco 49ers, 1994
Most pass receptions, season: 122, Chris Carter, Minnesota Vikings, 1994

Dynamite on Super Sunday

MIAMI, Fla., Jan. 29, 1995—Records came in bushels tonight as the San Francisco 49ers demolished the San Diego Chargers, 49–26, in Super Bowl XXIX.

San Francisco's Steve Young wound up with the highest quarter-back rating in a season in 1994. *Wide World*

There was Steve Young breaking Joe Montana's mark with six touchdown passes, Jerry Rice with a record three touchdown receptions that made him the leading scorer in Super Bowl history, and Rickey Waters standard-tying three touchdowns. In the process, the 49ers became the first team to win five Super Bowls.

Here are the major individual and team Super Bowl marks set in this lopsided, highest-scoring game:

Most points, career: 42, Jerry Rice, San Francisco 49ers, 3 games
Most points, game: 18, Jerry Rice, San Francisco 49ers, vs. Denver
Broncos, 1900 (3-td); vs. San Diego Chargers, 1995 (3-td); Ricky

145

Waters, San Francisco 49ers, vs. San Diego Chargers, 1995 (3-td) Ties Roger Craig, San Francisco 49ers, vs. Miami Dolphins, 1985 (3-td)

Most touchdowns, career: 7, Jerry Rice, San Francisco 49ers; 3 games (7-p)

Most touchdowns, game: 3, Jerry Rice, San Francisco 49ers, vs. San Diego Chargers, 1995 (3-p); vs. Denver Broncos, 1990 (3-p); Ricky Waters, San Francisco 49ers, vs. San Diego Chargers, 1995 (1-run-2-p) Ties Roger Craig, San Francisco 49ers, vs. Miami Dolphins, 1985 (1-run, 2-p)

Most touchdown passes, game: 6, Steve Young, San Francisco 49ers, vs. San Diego Chargers, 1995

Most points, both teams, game: 75 San Francisco 49ers (49), San Diego Chargers (26), 1995

Long-Distance Packer

CHICAGO, Ill., Sept. 11, 1995—Robert Brooks, the Green Bay Packers' wide receiver cast as the replacement for Sterling Sharpe, added a twist to his performance tonight against the Chicago Bears.

He scored on a record-tying 99-yard pass play (Brett Favre was the thrower) that gave the Packers a 21–0 lead, and added another TD reception that led to a 27–24 Green Bay victory.

Most yards on a completed pass: 99, Robert Brooks, Green Bay Packers, vs. Chicago Bears, Sept. 11, 1995 (Ties Frank Filchock to Andy Farkas, Washington Redskins, vs. Pittsburgh Steelers, Oct. 15, 1939; George Izo to Bobby Mitchell, Washington Redskins, vs. Cleveland Browns, Sept. 15, 1963; Karl Sweetan to Pat Studstill, Detroit Lions, vs. Baltimore Colts, Oct. 16, 1966; Sonny Jurgensen to Gerry Allen, Washington Redskins, vs. Chicago Bears, Sept. 15, 1968; Jim Plunkett to Cliff Branch, Los Angeles Raiders, vs. Washington Redskins, Oct. 2, 1983; Ron Jaworski to Mike Quick, Philadelphia Eagles, vs. Atlanta Falcons, Nov. 10, 1985; Bobby Humphries to Tony Martin, San Diego Chargers, vs. Seattle Seahawks, Sept. 18, 1994)

A Bootlegger's Run to Daylight

TEMPE, Ariz., Oct. 1, 1995—In his decade-old career Steve Bono had never etched his name in the NFL record book. But today the Kansas City Chiefs' quarterback made it—on a bootleg play.

Kansas City's Steve Bono made an unexpected entry into the NFL records against Arizona in 1995.   *Wide World*

On a fake handoff to Marcus Allen, he fooled the Arizona Cardinals' defense and ran, untouched, down the sideline for a shocking 76-yard touchdown. That started the Chiefs on the way to a 24–3 victory.

The 6-foot 4-inch, 215-pound Bono broke the 66-yard mark for longest touchdown run by a quarterback set by the Los Angeles Rams' Billy Wade against the Baltimore Colts on Dec. 11, 1960. Bono's feat also tied the Detroit Lions' Greg Landry for longest run by a quarterback.

Longest run for a touchdown by a quarterback: 76 yards, Steve Bono, Kansas City Chiefs, vs. Arizona Cardinals, Oct. 1, 1995
Longest run by a quarterback: 76 yards, Steve Bono, Kansas City Chiefs, vs. Arizona Cardinals, Oct. 1, 1995 (Ties Greg Landry, Detroit Lions, vs. Green Bay Packers, Sept. 20, 1970)

The Magnificent Monk

CHICAGO, Ill., Dec. 24, 1995—It didn't change the outcome of the game. It was one pass, good for 36 yards, that Art Monk caught today and it kept his streak alive in the final game of the season.

While the Chicago Bears beat the playoff-bound Philadelphia Eagles, 20–14, Monk extended his NFL record to 183 consecutive games with at least one pass reception. Signed by the Eagles late in the season, the celebrated wide receiver played 14 years with the Washington Redskins and one with the New York Jets last year.

Most consecutive games, pass receptions: 183, Art Monk 1995; Washington Redskins, 1980–93; New York Jets, 1994; Philadelphia Eagles, 1995

Catching Glory

ATLANTA, Ga., Dec. 24, 1995—It was another record day for the San Francisco 49ers' Jerry Rice, but the Atlanta Falcons spoiled it when they nipped the 49ers, 28–27, to gain a playoff berth in a season finale.

Art Monk caught most of the passes in his record streak with the
Washington Redskins.   *Wide World*

Rice was his usual brilliant self, scoring on a fumble recovery in the end zone and catching 12 passes for 153 yards. That gave him 122 for 1,848 yards in 16 games and enabled him to break the mark of 1,746 set by the Houston Oilers' Charlie Hennigan in a 14-game AFL season in 1961. He also established an NFL career mark for receptions at 942, two more than the Philadelphia Eagles' Art Monk, who caught one pass today against the Bears.

Rice's touchdown, the 155th of his career, added to his record total. Among his other marks, he also owns the league standard for career receiving touchdowns at 146.

San Francisco (11–5) had previously clinched the NFC Western Division crown. Atlanta (9–7) wound up second in the same division.

Most touchdowns, career: 155 (8-run, 1-fumble, 146-p), Jerry Rice, San Francisco 49ers, 1985–95

Most touchdowns on pass receptions, career: 146, Jerry Rice, San Francisco 49ers, 1985–95

Most receptions, career: 942, Jerry Rice, San Francisco 49ers, 1985–95

Most yards, season: 1,848, Jerry Rice, San Francisco 49ers, 1995

The Most of Shula

ST. LOUIS, Mo., Dec. 24, 1995—For Don Shula of the Miami Dolphins, today's 41–22 triumph over the St. Louis Rams could spell the end of an era.

After 26 seasons (33 overall in the NFL) as the team's jut-jawed head coach, the 65-year-old Shula has amassed a record 347 victories through this regular-season finale. And predictions were that he would step down after the playoffs.

In an unparalleled career that began when he became the youngest head coach in NFL history at age 33 with the Baltimore Colts, Shula in 1993 broke the league record for victories set at 324 by the Chicago Bears' George Halas.

Along the way, his teams in Baltimore and Miami appeared in six Super Bowls, winning twice, and he

The Miami Dolphins hoisted coach Don Shula after he broke the record for most victories in 1993. *Wide World*

became the only coach to guide a team through an unbeaten season and postseason when the Dolphins went 17-0 in 1972. His regular-season record: 347–172–6.

Most victories, coaching: 347, Don Shula, Baltimore Colts (1963–69), Miami Dolphins (1970–95)

Marino Magic

ST. LOUIS, Mo., Dec. 24, 1995—Adding to his assorted records, Dan Marino threw two touchdown passes today as the Miami Dolphins routed the St. Louis Rams, 41–22, in a regular-season finale.

A month ago, against the Indianapolis Colts, he passed for four touchdowns to break the 24-year-old career mark of 342 TD passes held by Fran Tarkenton. With today's performance, Marino wound up with 352.

The 13-year Dolphin also extended his NFL records

for most yards passing (48,841), completed passes (3,913), and most passes attempted (6,531).

Most touchdown passes, career: 352, Dan Marino, Miami Dolphins, 1983–95

Most yards gained passing, career: 48,841, Dan Marino, Miami Dolphins, 1983–95

Most passes completed, career: 3,913, Dan Marino, Miami Dolphins, 1983–95

Most passes attempted, career: 6,531, Dan Marino, Miami Dolphins, 1983–95

Miami's Dan Marino added to his many marks against the St. Louis Rams in the 1995 finale.   *Wide World*

Smithian Smash

TEMPE, Ariz., Dec. 25, 1995—Emmitt Smith eclipsed a mighty mark tonight as the Dallas Cowboys walloped the Arizona Cardinals, 37–13.

The 5-foot 9-inch, 203-pound running back scored his 25th touchdown of the season on a three-yard run with 5:49 remaining in the game. It broke the record of 24 set by the Washington Redskins' John Riggin in 1983.

It was Smith's 100th touchdown in a Cowboy career that began in 1990 and it tied him for ninth with Franco Harris on the career NFL list.

Most touchdowns, season: 25, Emmitt Smith, Dallas Cowboys, 1995

Dallas' Emmitt Smith now owns the record for most touchdowns in a season. *Wide World*

Cowboy Roundup

TEMPE, Ariz., Jan. 28, 1996—It wasn't the Cowboy stampede some had predicted, but Dallas held off the rallying Pittsburgh Steelers last night to win Super Bowl XXX, 27–17, in Sun Devil Stadium.

In a game that wound up with unsung Cowboy cornerback Larry Brown as MVP, two major individual Super Bowl records were set and a team record was tied.

While becoming the first team to win three titles in four years, Dallas joined San Francisco as the only franchises with five Super Bowl wins. And 32-year-old defensive end Charles Haley made history by becoming the first player to finger five Super Bowl rings.

Even though Emmitt Smith could muster only 49 yards on 18 carries, he scored two touchdowns on runs of one and four yards, giving him a record total of five TDs in Super Bowl competition. He scored the other three against the Buffalo Bills (one in XXVII, two in XXVIII). His five erased the mark shared by Pittsburgh's Franco Harris, San Francisco's Roger Craig, San Francisco's Jerry Rice, and Buffalo's Thurman Thomas.

Brown was voted MVP as a result of his two interceptions of Neil O'Donnell passes, the second one shattering Steeler hopes with 4:01 left in the game.

Super Bowl
Most victories, team: 5, Dallas Cowboys, VI, XII, XXVII, XXVIII, XXX (Ties San Francisco 49ers, XVI, XIX, XXIII, XXIV, XXIX)
Most touchdowns: 5, Emmitt Smith, Dallas Cowboys, XXVIII, XXX
Most Super Bowl rings: 5, Charles Haley, San Francisco 49ers, XXIV, XXIX; Dallas Cowboys, XXVIII, XXX

PRO BASKETBALL

Carom King

PHILADELPHIA, Pa., Nov. 24, 1960—Disappointing a Thanksgiving Day capacity crowd of 11,003 at Convention Hall, the Boston Celtics strengthened their hold on first place today by beating the Philadelphia Warriors, 132–129. But you certainly can't fault the Warriors' big Wilt Chamberlain, who hauled down a record 55 rebounds and scored 34 points, despite being guarded by defensive ace Bill Russell. Chamberlain's efforts off the backboards surpassed Russell's NBA record of 51 rebounds grabbed in a game against Syracuse last season.

Most rebounds, game: 55, Wilt Chamberlain, Philadelphia Warriors, vs. Boston Celtics, Nov. 24, 1960

All-Star Boardman

ST. LOUIS, Mo., Jan. 16, 1962—Playing before the hometown fans, Bob Pettit of the St. Louis Hawks grabbed a record 27 rebounds and scored 25 points as he led the West to a 150–130 victory tonight in the NBA All-Star Game. Pettit was chosen Most Valuable Player in this annual game for the fourth time, getting the nod over Wilt Chamberlain, who scored a record 42 points in a losing cause for the East.

Pettit had held both the former rebound record of 26 and the old scoring record of 29 points. The 6-foot 9-inch Hawk forward out of Louisiana State had good support in the West triumph as the Lakers' Elgin Baylor scored 32 points and Jerry West contributed 18. Cincinnati's Oscar Robertson added 26 points for the winners, while Walt Bellamy, a Chicago rookie, scored 23.

Most rebounds, NBA All-Star Game: 27, Bob Pettit, St. Louis Hawks, Jan. 16, 1962

Most points, NBA All-Star Game: 42, Wilt Chamberlain, Philadelphia Warriors, Jan. 16, 1962

Most times MVP, NBA All-Star Game: 4, Bob Pettit, 1956, 1958, 1959 (with Elgin Baylor), 1962

Bob Pettit of the St. Louis Hawks was a four-time All-Star Game MVP.   *UPI*

A 100 High

HERSHEY, Pa., March 2, 1962—The Big Dipper shone tonight as Wilt Chamberlain rewrote the record book by scoring 100 points against the New York Knickerbockers in a regular-season NBA game played here as one of the Philadelphia Warriors' "home" games.

The 7-foot 1-inch Chamberlain, who attended Overbrook High School in Philadelphia before going to the University of Kansas, established single-game records for most points, most field goals, most free throws made, and most shots, among others.

Chamberlain made his first 10 shots from the charity line and converted on a 28-of-32 overall to go with his 36-for-63 shooting from the field in a game easily won by the Warriors, 169–147.

Despite the defensive efforts of center Darrell Imhoff, forwards Cleveland Buckner and Willie Naulls, and just

Teammates and fans congratulate Philadelphia Warrior Wilt Chamberlain after he scored 100 points against the New York Knickerbockers.   Wide World

about everybody else on the Knick team, Chamberlain opened up with 23 points in the first quarter, had 41 at the half, and 69 when the third period ended. In the fourth quarter his teammates began feeding him consistently so that he could break his own record of 78 points scored earlier this season. The final two points came on a dunk shot with 46 seconds remaining in the game.

Most points, game: 100, Wilt Chamberlain, Philadelphia Warriors, vs. New York Knickerbockers, March 2, 1962

Most field goals attempted, game: 63, Wilt Chamberlain, Philadelphia Warriors, vs. New York Knickerbockers, March 2, 1962

Most field goals made, game: 36, Wilt Chamberlain, Philadelphia Warriors, vs. N.Y. Knickerbockers, March 2, 1962

Most free throws made, game: 28, Wilt Chamberlain, Philadelphia Warriors, vs. N.Y. Knickerbockers, March 2, 1962

Most points, half: 59, Wilt Chamberlain, Philadelphia Warriors, vs. N.Y. Knickerbockers, March 2, 1962

Making a Point

CHICAGO, Ill., March 14, 1962—Wilt Chamberlain, who set a rebounding record last season, finished this year with a 34-point performance that gave him 4,029 points and a 50.4-point-per-game scoring average as he led the Philadelphia Warriors to a 119–115 decision today over the expansion Chicago Packers.

The 7-foot Chamberlain, who created the NBA record of 2,149 rebounds during the 1960–61 campaign, was a scoring phenom this year as he set records for the most field goal attempts, most field goals made, most free throws attempted, in addition to his total points and scoring average. In one game this year, against the New York Knicks, he scored a record high 100 points.

Most points, season: 4,029, Wilt Chamberlain, Philadelphia Warriors, 1961–62

Highest scoring average, season: 50.4, Wilt Chamberlain, Philadelphia Warriors, 1961–62

Most field goals attempted, season: 3,159, Wilt Chamberlain, Philadelphia Warriors, 1961–62

Most field goals made, season: 1,597, Wilt Chamberlain, Philadelphia Warriors, 1961–62

Most free throws attempted, season: 1,363, Wilt Chamberlain, Philadelphia Warriors, 1961–62

Most rebounds, season: 2,149, Wilt Chamberlain, Philadelphia Warriors, 1960–61

Sweet Charity

LOS ANGELES, Cal., March 20, 1966—Jerry West converted 11 of 12 free throws as he scored 35 points in leading Los Angeles to a 124–112 victory over the San Francisco Warriors tonight. The loss prevented the Warriors from gaining a playoff berth in the NBA's Western Division.

The 6-foot 3-inch West, a six-year pro out of West Virginia University, created an NBA record with his free-throw shooting. The 11 tonight raised his total for the season to 840, breaking the old mark of 835 set by Wilt Chamberlain four seasons ago. West, who is called "Zeke from Cabin Creek," averaged 28.7 points a game this season.

Most free throws made, season: 840, Jerry West, Los Angeles Lakers, 1965–66

Deadly

SYRACUSE, N.Y., Feb. 28, 1967—Wilt Chamberlain made his first four shots from the floor before he missed a whirling underhanded layup, ending a record 35-for-35 field-goal shooting streak. Wilt went on to score 28 points tonight in leading the Philadelphia 76ers past Cincinnati, 127–107. The 76ers played in this upstate New York city for 15 seasons as the Syracuse Nationals before transferring to Philadelphia four years ago.

Chamberlain's shooting streak began 11 days ago against this same Cincinnati team in a 127–118 Philadelphia victory in Cleveland. The highlight of the

The Los Angeles Lakers' Jerry West lines up for his 840th successful free throw, a single-season standard. *UPI*

streak, however, came a week ago when the Big Dipper dropped in 11 shots in 11 attempts in taking the 76ers to a 123–122 victory over St. Louis.

Most consecutive field goals: 35, Wilt Chamberlain, Philadelphia 76ers, Feb. 17, 1967, to Feb. 28, 1967

End of Laker Chain

MILWAUKEE, Wis., Jan. 9, 1972—The team defense of the Milwaukee Bucks and the individual brilliance of Kareem Abdul-Jabbar brought an end to the longest winning streak in major professional sports. Milwaukee defeated the Los Angeles Lakers, 120–104, before a sellout crowd of 10,746 and a national television audience this afternoon, ending the Lakers' 33-game string that began on Oct. 31, 1971.

The defeat came about because Milwaukee guards Lucius Allen, Oscar Robertson, Jon McGlocklin, and Wali Jones kept rushing back on defense, cutting off the Lakers' fast break. Los Angeles had used the rebounding of Wilt Chamberlain and Happy Hairston and the quickness of Jerry West, Gail Goodrich, Jim Price and Jim McMillan to run their way to victory in most of the 33 triumphs.

In addition to the defense by the Buck backcourt, Milwaukee center Kareem Abdul-Jabbar, the former Lew Alcindor, outplayed Chamberlain in the pivot and outfought Hairston under the boards as he scored 39 points and pulled down 20 rebounds.

Most consecutive victories: 33, Los Angeles Lakers, Oct. 31, 1971, to Jan. 7, 1972

Milwaukee's Kareem Abdul-Jabbar lofts one over Wilt Chamberlain as the Bucks end the Lakers' 33-game winning streak. *UPI*

The Last Dip

OAKLAND, Cal., March 25, 1973—Wilt Chamberlain, who apparently can do anything he wants to do with a basketball when he puts his mind to it, took his first shot at the basket in 75 minutes of playing time over a two-game span. It was his only shot of the night, and he missed it, but the Los Angeles Lakers won this final game of the season over the Golden State Warriors, 96–89.

The Big Dipper, playing the last regular-season game of his career, scored one point on a free throw, pulled down 18 rebounds, and passed for nine assists. In his next-to-last game, against the Milwaukee Bucks, Chamberlain failed to take any shots at all from the field.

Throughout his career, the 7-foot 1-inch center has been something of a puzzle, although no one has ever questioned his ability. After leading the league in scoring and becoming MVP in his first year, 1959–60, with the Philadelphia Warriors, Chamberlain followed the next season by setting a mark for rebounds (2,149) that still stands. In 1961–62 he shattered all sorts of records en route to a 14-year career that included championships with the Philadelphia 76ers in 1967 and the Lakers in 1972.

He owns many of the league's career offensive records, among other marks, and he has the added distinction of never having fouled out of a game.

Most seasons and most consecutive seasons leading league in scoring: 7, Wilt Chamberlain, Philadelphia Warriors, 1959–62; San Francisco Warriors, 1962–64; San Francisco Warriors–Philadelphia 76ers, 1964–65; Philadelphia 76ers, 1965–66

Most games, 50 or more points, career: 118, Wilt Chamberlain, Philadelphia Warriors, 1959–62; San Francisco Warriors, 1962–64; San Francisco Warriors–Philadelphia 76ers, 1964–65; Philadelphia 76ers, 1965–68; Los Angeles Lakers, 1968–73

Most seasons and most consecutive seasons leading league in field goals: 7, Wilt Chamberlain, Philadelphia Warriors, 1959–62; San Francisco Warriors, 1962–64; San Francisco Warriors–Philadelphia 76ers, 1964–65; Philadelphia 76ers, 1965–66

Among his many achievements, Wilt Chamberlain never fouled out of a game. *UPI*

Most seasons leading league in rebounds: 11, Wilt Chamberlain, Philadelphia Warriors, 1959–62; San Francisco Warriors, 1962–63; Philadelphia 76ers, 1965–68; Los Angeles Lakers, 1968–69, 1970–73

Most rebounds, career: 23,924. Wilt Chamberlain, Philadelphia Warriors, 1959–62; San Francisco Warriors, 1962–65; Philadelphia 76ers, 1964–68; Los Angeles Lakers, 1968–73

Longest Shot

SAN ANTONIO, Tex., Jan. 19, 1977—It happened late in the first half of the game tonight between the Chicago Bulls and the San Antonio Spurs.

Artis Gilmore gathered in a rebound for Chicago and handed off to Norm Van Lier, who was under the basket. Van Lier uncorked a hook shot that traveled the length of the court and swished through the basket. It was measured as an 84-footer, the longest basket in NBA history.

Ironically, those were Van Lier's only two points of the night as the Bulls were beaten by the Spurs, 115–107.

Longest basket: 84 feet, Norm Van Lier, Chicago Bulls, Jan. 19, 1977

Pure Calvin

SAN ANTONIO, Tex., March 29, 1981—Although San Antonio defeated Houston, 135–109, tonight, there was a high note sounded for little Calvin Murphy of the Rockets. His 4-for-4 from the free-throw line enabled him to finish the season with a .958 free-throw percentage, an NBA record.

Houston's Calvin Murphy was a little guy who stood tall on the free-throw line. *Ron Modra*

The 5-foot 9-inch Murphy, one of the finest pure shooters in the game, registered 78 consecutive free throws early in the season.

Highest free-throw percentage, season: .958, Calvin Murphy, Houston Rockets, 1980–81

Randy on a Roll

DALLAS, Tex., March 13, 1983—He got to play only four minutes in the second half and went 2-for-2 for four points today as the Dallas Mavericks beat the San Diego Clippers, 111–102.

For Randy Smith, the durable Clipper guard, it was an insignificant finale to a monumental streak that had begun when he was with the Buffalo Braves on Feb. 18, 1972. Since then, playing for the Braves, the Clippers, the Cleveland Cavaliers, the New York Knickerbockers, and the Clippers once more, Smith never missed a game.

It all added up to 906 consecutive games, an NBA record, and it ended when Smith was given his release.

Although Smith's is the NBA standard, Ron Boone can lay claim to the longest all-time pro mark. Boone, a guard who played for six teams in the American Basketball Association and NBA, appeared in 1,041 consecutive games from 1968 to 1981.

Most consecutive games played, NBA: 906, Randy Smith, Buffalo Braves, San Diego Clippers, Cleveland Cavaliers, New York Knickerbockers, San Diego Clippers, Feb. 18, 1972—March 13, 1983
Most consecutive games played, ABA-NBA: 1,041, Ron Boone, Dallas Chaparrals, Utah Stars, St. Louis Spirits, Kansas City Kings, Los Angeles Lakers, Utah Jazz, Oct. 31, 1968—Jan. 24, 1981

Buckets by the Bushel

DENVER, Col., Dec. 13, 1983—Colorado, famous for its mountain country, reached a new peak tonight when the Detroit Pistons defeated the Denver Nuggets,

186–184, in a triple-overtime game. It was the highest-scoring NBA game in history.

Guards Isiah Thomas, with 47 points, and John Long, 41, sparked the Pistons, and forwards Kiki Vandeweghe, with 51, and Alex English, 47, paced the Nuggets. The game was tied at 145 at the end of regulation time.

The 370-point total broke the record of 337 set by San Antonio (171) and Milwaukee (166) in three overtimes on March 6, 1982. It also erased the all-time pro mark of 342 points recorded in the ABA by the San Diego Conquistadors (176) and the New York Nets (166) on February 14, 1975. That one took four overtimes and featured a 63-point performance by the Nets' Julius Erving.

Most points scored, both teams, one game: 360, Detroit Pistons (186) vs. Denver Nuggets (184), Dec. 13, 1983

Best Bet

LAS VEGAS, Nev., Jan. 4, 1984—Even in this betting capital of the world there were no odds given for Adrian Dantley's chances of breaking Wilt Chamberlain's NBA mark of 28 free throws made in one game.

Well, the Utah Jazz's star forward didn't break it tonight; he tied it. Of his 46 points in the 116–111 victory over the Houston Rockets, Dantley scored 28 on fouls. He missed only one foul shot, the difference between tying and snapping Chamberlain's 22-year-old record.

Most free throws made, game: 28, Adrian Dantley, Utah Jazz, vs. Houston Rockets, Jan. 4, 1984 (Ties Wilt Chamberlain, Philadelphia Warriors, vs. New York Knickerbockers, March 2, 1962)

Great Scott!

BOSTON, Mass., May 27, 1985—Scott Wedman, the 11-year pro veteran who serves as a swingman for the Boston Celtics, had the shooting day of a lifetime today as the Celtics routed the Los Angeles Lakers, 148–114, in the opening game of the championship series.

Wedman hit 11-for-11 from the floor, including four three-pointers—three in succession—to set an NBA playoff record.

The 33-year-old Wedman, a product of Colorado University who played for seven years with the Kansas City Kings, then with the Cleveland Cavaliers before joining the Celtics in 1982–83, registered a total of 26 points, which tied teammate Kevin McHale for scoring honors. He played 23 minutes.

Most consecutive field goals, game, championship series: 11, Scott Wedman, Boston Celtics, May 27, 1985

Here Comes Mr. Jordan

BOSTON, Mass., April 20, 1986—Michael Jordan, the airborne sensation of the Chicago Bulls, scored a playoff-record 63 points today against the Boston Celtics.

Despite his heroics, the Celtics won in double over-time, 135–131, to give them a 2–0 advantage in the opening-round series.

Jordan, the 6-foot 6-inch leaping lizard out of North Carolina, hit on 22 of 41 shots from the field and made 19 of his 21 attempts from the foul line.

He broke Elgin Baylor's playoff mark of 61, set by the Los Angeles Laker against the Celtics in the 1962 championship series.

Most points, NBA playoffs, game: 63, Michael Jordan, Chicago Bulls, vs. Boston Celtics, April 20, 1986

Chicago's Michael Jordan soared into the record book in the 1986 playoffs. *Chicago Bulls/SPS*

Detroit's Isiah Thomas stole a record in the 1988 championship series.
Ira Golden

On the Steal

LOS ANGELES, Cal., June 21, 1988—Isiah Thomas wound up with a playoff record tonight, but it was small solace as the Lakers overcame the Detroit Pistons, 103–102, to win Game 7 and their second NBA championship in a row.

The peerless Piston, hobbled by a sprained ankle, managed to score 43 points and added fours steals, giving him a record 20 steals for a 7-game championship series.

Earlier, in the Western Conference semifinals, Utah's John Stockton posted a record 28 steals for a 7-game series, against the Lakers.

Most steals, 7-game championship series: 20, Isiah Thomas, Detroit Pistons, vs. Los Angeles Lakers, 1988

Kareem Abdul-Jabbar's 20 years in the NBA produced a basket of records. *Vic Milton*

Ode to Jabbar

LOS ANGELES, Cal., April 23, 1989—His son, Amir, sang the National Anthem, his teammates gave him a Rolls Royce and team owner Jerry Buss contributed a tennis court at his Kauai home.

It was all part of the farewell ceremonies at the final regular-season game tonight for super-center Kareem Abdul-Jabbar of the Los Angeles Lakers. What he did—10 points, 3 assists, 6 rebounds—in the 121–117 victory over the Denver Nuggets merely added to the battery of all-time NBA marks he has amassed.

The 7-foot 2-inch Jabbar, who came out of New York City and UCLA to play six years with the Milwaukee Bucks and 14 with the Lakers, left the game with career records for most seasons, most games, most minutes played, most points, most field goals, most field-goal attempts, most defensive rebounds, most personal fouls, and most blocked shots, among other regular and post-season marks.

Most minutes, career: 57,446, Kareem Abdul-Jabbar, Milwaukee Bucks, 1969–75; Los Angeles Lakers, 1975–89

Most points, career: 38,387, Kareem Abdul-Jabbar, Milwaukee Bucks, 1969–75; Los Angeles Lakers, 1975–89

Most field goals, career: 15,837, Kareem Abdul-Jabbar, Milwaukee Bucks, 1969–75; Los Angeles Lakers, 1975–89

Most field goal attempts, career: 28,307, Kareem Abdul-Jabbar, Milwaukee Bucks, 1969–75; Los Angeles Lakers, 1975–89

Most defensive rebounds, career: 9,394, Kareem Abdul-Jabbar, Milwaukee Bucks, 1969–75; Los Angeles Lakers, 1975–89

Most defensive rebounds, season: 1,111, Kareem Abdul-Jabbar, Los Angeles Lakers, 1975–76

Most defensive rebounds, game: 29, Kareem Abdul-Jabbar, Los Angeles Lakers, vs. Detroit Pistons, Dec. 14, 1975

Tying Magic

LOS ANGELES, Cal., May 17, 1988—John Stockton's Utah Jazz lost the game, 111–109, to the Los Angeles Lakers tonight, but the peerless guard tied a playoff record in the process.

Stockton posted 24 assists to equal the mark set by the Los Angeles Lakers' Magic Johnson against the Phoenix Suns on May 15, 1984.

The Lakers took a 3-to-2 lead in this Western Conference semifinal when Michael Cooper sank his only field goal of the game with seven seconds remaining.

Most assists, game, playoffs: 24, John Stockton, Utah Jazz, vs. Los Angeles Lakers, May 17, 1988 (Ties Magic Johnson, Los Angeles Lakers, vs. Phoenix Suns, May 15, 1984)

Skiles' Skills

ORLANDO, Fla., Dec. 30, 1990—Scott Skiles, a 6-foot 1-inch guard, set an NBA record with 30 assists tonight when he led the Orlando Magic to a 155–116 victory over the Denver Nuggets.

The former Michigan State All-American, now in his fifth year in the NBA, eclipsed the mark of 29 assists set by New Jersey's Kevin Porter against Houston in 1978.

Skiles also scored 22 points, 13 in a fourth-quarter blitz.

Most assists, game: 30, Scott Skiles, Orlando Magic, vs. Denver Nuggets, Dec. 30, 1990

A Cheer with a Tear

OAKLAND, Cal., April 21, 1991—Even though he had cause for celebration, Utah's John Stockton was less than jubilant tonight after the Golden State Warriors drubbed the Jazz, 125–106, in a regular-season finale.

The Jazz guard's 11 assists gave him a total of 1,164 for the season, the most in NBA annals. This broke the mark of 1,134 that Stockton set last year.

But Golden State's victory denied Utah (54–28) the Western Division title, which went to the San Antonio Spurs (55–27).

Most assists, season: 1,164, John Stockton, Utah Jazz, 1990–91

A Foul Streak

SAN ANTONIO, Tex., Nov. 9, 1993—It all ended with little ceremony. Micheal Williams of the Minnesota Timberwolves sunk his first two foul shots tonight against the San Antonio Spurs. And then the inevitable happened. He missed the next one.

So Williams' streak would go into the NBA record book as 97 successful free throws in a row. He had begun it late last season and in less than a month he'd snapped the mark of 78 straight by the Houston Rockets' Calvin Murphy. By the end of the year he also owned the season record of 84 in a row.

San Antonio prevailed in today's game, 110–95, but the result couldn't dim the achievement of this deadeye from the line.

Most consecutive free throws made, season: 84, Micheal Williams, Minnesota Timberwolves, March 24, 1993—April 25, 1993
Most consecutive free throws made: 97, Micheal Williams, Minnesota Timberwolves, March 24, 1993–Nov. 9, 1993

Trey Bien

WASHINGTON, D.C., April 23, 1995—Dana Barros, a small package who can hit from way out, ended his season today with a three-point shooting record.

The 5-foot 11-inch, 163-pound 76er sank two three-pointers, marking his 58th consecutive game with at least one trey, as the Washington Bullets downed Philadelphia, 106–90.

On March 25, against Indiana, Barros broke the record previously set at 43 by the Denver Nuggets' Michael Adams in 1988.

Most consecutive games, three-point field goals made: 58, Dana Barros, Philadelphia 76ers, Dec. 23, 1994—April 23, 1995

The Helping Hand

SALT LAKE CITY, Utah, April 20, 1996—Utah's John Stockton finished a record season tonight in the Jazz 104–92 victory over the Sacramento Kings.

His four assists and one steal boosted the nonpareil guard's career marks to 3,386 assists and 2,365 steals. In addition, he won the assist title for the ninth consecutive season, breaking the record he had shared with the Boston Celtics' Bob Cousy.

On Feb. 1, 1995, against the Denver Nuggets, Stockton toppled the assist record of 9,921 set by the Los Angeles Lakers' Magic Johnson. This season, on Feb. 20, against the Boston Celtics, he erased the steals mark of 2,311 posted by Maurice Cheeks, who made his with the Philadelphia 76ers, New York Knickerbockers, San Antonio Spurs, Atlanta Hawks, and New Jersey Nets.

Most assists career: 3,386, John Stockton, Utah Jazz, 1984–85—1995–96

Most steals, career: 2,365, John Stockton, Utah Jazz, 1984–85—1995–96

Most consecutive seasons, leading league, assists: 9, John Stockton, Utah Jazz, 1987–88—1995–96

Assists are synonymous with Utah's John Stockton, who adds to his records every time he takes the court.   *Wide World*

The Shooter and the Ageless One

CHARLOTTE, N.C., April 21, 1996—Orlando's 27-year-old Dennis Scott and Charlotte's 42-year-old Robert Parish wound up record seasons today in the Magic's 103–100 decision over the Hornets.

Scott made 11 three-point shots in a 35-point performance, giving him a single-season mark of 267 three-pointers. On March 19, against the Detroit Pistons, he erased the record of 217 treys set by the New York Knickerbockers' John Starks last season.

The Magic's sharpshooter also made a one-game record two nights ago with 11 three-pointers against the Atlanta Hawks. It surpassed by one the mark shared by the Miami Heat's Dennis Scott (now with the Magic) in

1993; the Detroit Pistons' Joe Dumars in 1994, and the Dallas Mavericks' George McCloud this season.

Today's game extended Parish's record to 1,568 appearances in his 20th season in the NBA. On April 6, he broke the mark of 1,560 games played, set by Kareem Abdul-Jabbar in 20 years with the Milwaukee Bucks and the Los Angeles Lakers. Parish also tied Abdul-Jabbar for most seasons.

Most three-point field goals, game: 11, Dennis Scott, Orlando Magic, vs. Atlanta Hawks, April 19, 1996

Most three-point field goals, career: 267, Dennis Scott, Orlando Magic, 1990–91—1995–96

Most games played: 1,568: Robert Parish, Golden State Warriors, 1976–77—1979–80; Boston Celtics, Charlotte Hornets, 1976–77—1995–96

Most seasons: 20, Robert Parish, Golden State Warriors, 1976–77—1979–80. Boston Celtics, 1980–81—1993–94; Charlotte Hornets, 1994–95—1995–96 (Ties Kareem Abdul-Jabbar, Milwaukee Bucks, 1969–70—1974–75; Los Angeles Lakers, 1975–76—1988–89)

Orlando's Dennis Scott shot from afar to achieve two records in 1995–96.   *Wide World*

Hakeem One-Ups Kareem

HOUSTON, Tex., April 21, 1996—Hakeem Olajuwon, the towering center of the Houston Rockets, deleted one of Kareem Abdul-Jabbar's mighty marks today in a season-ending 118–110 beating of the Phoenix Suns.

Olajuwon recorded no. 3,190 in blocked shots, one more than the total amassed by Jabbar in 20 seasons with the Milwaukee Bucks and Los Angeles Lakers. Olajuwon has played for 12 years.

Most blocked shots, career: 3,190, Hakeem Olajuwon, Houston Rockets, 1984–85—1995–96

The Bull Market

WASHINGTON, D.C., April 21, 1996—Fittingly, Michael Jordan, the reigning superstar, led the way as the Chicago Bulls wrapped up the most successful regular season in history today. Jordan's 26 points and Scottie Pippen's 20 enabled the Bulls to defeat the Washington Bullets, 103–93, for their 72nd victory.

In Milwaukee, on April 16, Chicago had become the winningest NBA team of all time when it held off the Milwaukee Bucks, 86–80, for no. 70. That broke the league mark of 69 set by the 1971–72 Los Angeles Lakers, who were headed by Wilt Chamberlain and Jerry West.

Most victories, season: 72, Chicago Bulls, 1995–96

HOCKEY

Goal-Getter

QUEBEC CITY, Quebec, Jan. 31, 1920—Joe Malone, who led the National Hockey League in scoring in its first season two years ago with 44 goals in 20 games, has another line in the record book. The new Quebec Bulldog, who came from the Montreal Canadiens at the beginning of the season, scored seven goals tonight against the Toronto St. Patricks, more goals than anyone has ever scored in a single NHL game. The Bulldogs beat Toronto, 10–6.

Most goals, game: 7, Joe Malone, Quebec Bulldogs, vs. Toronto St. Patricks, Jan. 31, 1920

Canadien Goose Eggs

MONTREAL, Quebec, March 14, 1929—Montreal Canadien goalie George Hainsworth recorded his 22nd shutout in 44 games as he held the Maroons scoreless in tonight's season closer. Howie Morenz scored the only goal as the Canadiens beat their intra-city rivals, 1–0.

Hainsworth's phenomenal goaltending—he allowed only 43 goals all season—is all the more surprising in view of a rule change implemented by the NHL this season that was supposed to introduce more offense into the game. The change allowed forward passing in all three zones, a team's defensive zone, the center

Former Canadien Joe Malone scored seven goals for the Quebec Bull-dogs against the Toronto St. Pats in 1920.   *Hockey Hall of Fame*

zone between the blue lines,* and in the attacking zone. Previously, no forward passing was allowed in the attacking zone.

Most shutouts, season: 22, George Hainsworth, Montreal Canadiens, 1928–29

*Editor's Note: The red line at center ice was not introduced until 1943.

Puck Stopper

NEW YORK, Feb. 1, 1970—Filling in for the injured Ed Giacomin, 40-year-old Terry Sawchuk was minding the nets for the New York Rangers tonight and he stopped 29 Pittsburgh shots to chalk up the 103rd shutout of his National Hockey League career as New York won, 6–0.

It was a memorable night on the Madison Square Garden ice as the Rangers' Dave Balon scored three goals for his first hat trick and Billy Fairbairn recorded three assists to establish a club scoring mark of 42 points by a rookie.

But the hero of the game was Sawchuk, Rookie of the Year 21 seasons ago, the only man ever to shut out more than 100 opposing teams. He did it with Detroit, the team he broke in with in 1949, Boston, Toronto, Los Angeles and the Rangers. This was Sawchuk's first shutout since the 1967–68 season, when he was with the Kings.

Most shutouts, NHL career: 103, Terry Sawchuk, Detroit Red Wings, 1949–55; Boston Bruins, 1955–57; Detroit Red Wings, 1957–64; Toronto Maple Leafs, 1964–67; Los Angeles Kings, 1967–68; Detroit Red Wings, 1968–69; New York Rangers, 1969–70

Tony Awards

CHICAGO, Ill., March 29, 1970—Squat, but mobile, Tony Esposito recorded the 15th shutout of this, his

Terry Sawchuck posted 85 of his 103 shutouts with the Detroit Red Wings.
Scotty Kilpatrick

rookie season, as the Chicago Blackhawks beat the Toronto Maple Leafs tonight, 4–0. Three days ago Esposito broke Harry Lumley's 16-year-old modern record with his 14th shutout of the season.

The modern era for goaltenders dates from the 1943–44 season when the red line at center ice was introduced.

This line had the effect of speeding up the game by adding more offense, since it allowed a player to pass the puck out of his own defensive zone. Previously the player would have to carry the puck out of the zone himself.

Nearing the end of a spectacular season, Esposito—whose brother Phil is a leading scorer with the Boston Bruins—should win both the Calder Trophy as Rookie of the Year and the Vezina Trophy as the league's best goaltender.

Most shutouts, season (modern): 15, Tony Esposito, Chicago Black-
hawks, 1969–70

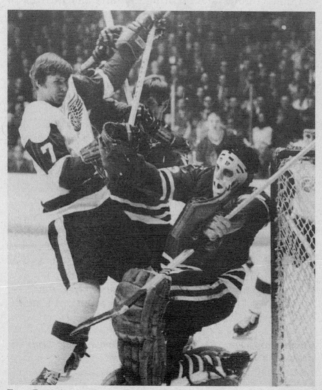

Tony Esposito set the modern mark of 15 shutouts in a season as a Blackhawks' goalie.   *UPI*

Flyers' Hammer

PHILADELPHIA, Pa., April 6, 1975—The Philadelphia Flyers' Hammer struck in an unusual manner tonight, scoring a goal and waiting until only eight minutes remained in the game before getting into a fight. The Hammer, as forward Dave Schultz is referred to by his Flyer teammates, scored a third-period goal—his ninth of the season—in helping Philadelphia to a 6–2 victory over Atlanta in the last game of the regular season.

Eight minutes after scoring, Schultz and Ed Kea of the Flames got into a fight and were sent to the penalty box with major and minor penalties, much to the delight of the 17,007 fans in the Spectrum, who love the Hammer's roughhouse tactics. The seven penalty minutes tonight gave Schultz a total of 472 for the season, far outdistancing the record 348 penalty minutes he accumulated last year in leading Philadelphia to the Stanley Cup championship.

Most penalty minutes, season: 472, Dave Schultz, Philadelphia Flyers, 1974–75

Sittler's Explosion

TORONTO, Ont., Feb. 7, 1976—Until tonight, Darryl Sittler was in a slump, having scored only five goals in the last 17 games. But the Toronto Maple Leaf center exploded with six goals (on 10 shots) and four assists in an 11–4 thumping of the Boston Bruins.

His 10 points smashed the one-game NHL mark set by Maurice "Rocket" Richard of the Montreal Canadiens in 1944 (five goals and three assists).

Most points, game: 10, Darryl Sittler, Toronto Maple Leafs, vs. Boston Bruins, Feb. 7, 1976 (six goals, four assists)

Philadelphia's David Schultz and his big stick added up to record penalties. *Wide World*

Here's Howe

HARTFORD, Conn., April 6, 1980—Fifty-two-year-old Gordie Howe ended his regular-season career tonight with a goal and an assist as the Hartford Whalers topped the Detroit Red Wings, 5–3.

In his 26th NHL season (there were six others in the World Hockey Association) the remarkable Methuselah of hockey added to a legend that began with the Detroit Red Wings in 1946–47.

He wound up with most goals (801) and career records for most seasons (26) and most games (1,767), among others.

Most seasons: 26, Gordie Howe, Detroit Red Wings, 1946–71; Hartford Whalers, 1979–80
Most games: 1,767, Gordie Howe, Detroit Red Wings, 1946–71; Hartford Whalers, 1979–80

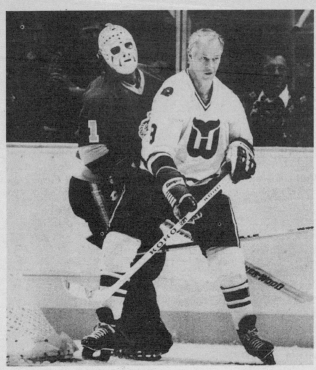

Gordie Howe ended his 26-year NHL career with the Hartford Whalers and a keg of records. *Wide World*

Marathon Man

HARTFORD, Conn., Oct. 10, 1987—Doug Jarvis played on four Stanley Cup championship teams with the Montreal Canadiens and won the Frank J. Selke Trophy as the best defensive forward in 1983–84 with the Washington Capitals. But he will be best remembered for an incredible streak that began with his first game as a Canadien in 1975.

In a career that took him to Washington in 1982 and to Hartford in 1985, Jarvis never missed a single game. Tonight, in his farewell appearance before a record home crowd of 15,203, he played his 964th consecutive game.

The New York Rangers beat the Whalers, 6–2, but it couldn't diminish Jarvis' iron-man mark. He had broken Garry Unger's record of 914 consecutive games on Dec. 25, 1986, when he played against the Canadiens, his original team.

Most consecutive games: 964, Doug Jarvis, Montreal Canadiens, Washington Capitals, Hartford Whalers, Oct. 8, 1975–Oct. 10, 1987

The Mark of a Tiger

HARTFORD, Conn., Feb. 11, 1988—Dave "Tiger" Williams didn't get his nickname because he was a pussy cat. A master of muscle and intimidation, the 5-foot 11-inch, 190-pound left wing was a menace on ice from his first days in the NHL with the 1974–75 Toronto Maple Leafs, and he never let up after moving on to Vancouver, Detroit, Los Angeles and, this season, Hartford.

But it all ended today when the pugnacious native of Saskatchewan was released by the Whalers. He left the sport with a record 3,966 penalty minutes in 962 games over 14 seasons. Overall, counting playoffs, Dave totaled 4,421 minutes in the penalty box.

Most penalty minutes, career, regular season: 3,966, Dave "Tiger" Williams, Toronto Maple Leafs, Vancouver Canucks, Detroit Red Wings, Los Angeles Kings, Hartford Whalers, 1974–75— 1987–88

The Mario Show

PITTSBURGH, Pa., April 25, 1989—Playing despite a neck injury that made it difficult to turn his head,

Mario Lemieux of the Pittsburgh Penguins put on a spectacular one-man show tonight against the Philadelphia Flyers.

He registered five goals and three assists to lead the Penguins to a 10–7 victory in the fifth game of the Patrick Division finals. The superstar center's eight points tied the single–game playoff record set in 1988 by Patrik Sundstrom of the New Jersey Devils against the Washington Capitals.

Most points, game, playoffs: 8 (five goals, three assists), Mario Lemieux, Pittsburgh Penguins, vs. Philadelphia Flyers, April 25, 1989 (Ties Patrik Sundstrom (three goals, five assists), New Jersey Devils, vs. Washington Capitals, April 22, 1988)

Pittsburgh's Mario Lemieux scored eight points in one game.
Bruce Bennett

A Hulluva Performance

ST. LOUIS, Mo., March 31, 1991—It may not have called for a champagne celebration—the Cup is yet to come—but St. Louis Blues fans had happy reason to toast their hero, Brett Hull.

With tonight's 2–1 victory over the Minnesota North Stars, Hull wrapped up his best offensive season. On the way to MVP laurels, Hull had set a record for most goals in a season by a right wing (86) and he'd become only the third player in NHL history to score 50 goals in fewer than 50 games.

Hull, who'd broken his own mark of 72, set last season, fell shy of center Wayne Gretzky's all-time record of 92.

Most goals by a right winger, season: 86, Brett Hull, St. Louis Blues, 1990–91

St. Louis' Brett Hull became a 70-goaler in 1990.   *Bruce Bennett*

Flight of the Penguins

PITTSBURGH, Pa., April 10, 1993—In 24 hours the Pittsburgh Penguins set an NHL mark with their 16th consecutive victory and then No. 17.

Last night Mario Lemieux scored five goals to lead the Penguins to a 10–4 swamping of the New York Rangers, though tonight at home he didn't score a goal as four teammates chipped in with goals to again chop down the Rangers, 4–2.

The high-flying Penguins first broke the record of the New York Islanders, who had won 15 straight games before capturing the Stanley Cup in 1981–82.

Most consecutive victories: 17, Pittsburgh Penguins, March 9, 1993–April 10, 1993

Check Bounced

NEW YORK, N.Y., May 5, 1993—NHL Commissioner Gary Bettman put the Washington Capitals' Dale Hunter into the record book today. And it was not for a proud achievement.

Bettman handed out the longest nondrug-related suspension in league history—21 games—to the 5-foot 10-inch, 200-pound center for his cheap-shot check on the New York Islanders' Pierre Turgeon in an April 28 playoff game.

It happened seconds after Turgeon scored the fifth goal in a 5–3 Patrick Division semfinal series-clinching victory. Hunter hit him from behind with a gloved hand to the face, sending Turgeon into the boards and resulting in a separated right shoulder.

In addition to all preseason games next season and the first 21 regular-season games, Hunter was fined one-fourth of his salary, which comes to about $150,000.

The previous longest suspension for an act of violence was 20 games, given the Chicago Blackhawks' Tom Lysiak for tripping a linesman in 1983.

Longest suspension: 21 games, Dale Hunter, Washington Capitals, May 4, 1993

Bondra's Barrage

WASHINGTON, Feb. 5, 1994—Peter Bondra broke out of a season-long slump tonight in a record way. The Russian-born right wing, who had only 14 goals in his previous 18 games, scored four goals in the first period and added a fifth in the Washington Capitals' 6–3 victory over the Tampa Bay Lightning. His first four goals tied a one-period NHL record shared now by 10 players.

Most goals, one period: 4, Peter Bondra, Washington Capitals, vs. Tampa Bay Lightning, Feb. 5, 1994 (Ties Harvey Jackson, Toronto Maple Leafs, vs. St. Louis Eagles, Nov. 20, 1934; Max Bentley, Chicago Blackhawks, vs. New York Rangers, Jan. 28, 1943; Clint Smith, Chicago Blackhawks, vs. Montreal Canadiens, March 4, 1945; Red Berenson, St. Louis Blues, vs. Philadelphia Flyers, Nov. 7, 1968; Wayne Gretzky, Edmonton Oilers, vs. St. Louis Blues, Feb. 18, 1981; Grant Mulvey, Chicago Blackhawks, vs. St. Louis Blues, Feb. 3, 1982; Bryan Trottier, New York Islanders, vs. Philadelphia Flyers, Feb. 13, 1982; Al Secord, Chicago Blackhawks, vs. Toronto Maple Leafs, Jan. 7, 1987; Joe Nieuwendyk, Calgary Flames, vs. Winnipeg Jets, Jan. 11, 1989)

The Great Gretzky

CHICAGO, Ill., April 14, 1996—He didn't score and he didn't get an assist today as the St. Louis Blues tied the Chicago Blackhawks, 2–2, in a regular-season finale.

But for the Blues' Wayne Gretzky it was a season in which he switched teams and added to the harvest of records made in an incredible 17-year career.

Originally the spectacular force behind the Edmonton Oilers, "The Great Gretzky" was traded to the Los Angeles Kings in the summer of 1988. And this year he joined the Blues on Feb. 27.

Along the way, this nonpareil center has set records by winning the scoring title nine times and the Hart (MVP) Trophy nine times, and he captained the Edmonton Oilers to four Stanley Cup championships.

But the most memorable moment came on the night of March 23, 1994, when he became the league's career-leading goal-scorer with No. 802, passing Gordie Howie. Through today's game, he had 837 goals.

You could fill a book with all his marks. What follows are a partial listing of the major ones:

Regular Season

Most goals, career: 837, Wayne Gretzky, Edmonton Oilers, Los Angeles Kings, St. Louis Blues, 1979–80—1994–96

Most assists, career: 1,771, Wayne Gretzky, Edmonton Oilers, Los Angeles Kings, 1979–80—1994–95

Most points, career: 2,608, Wayne Gretzky, Edmonton Oilers, Los Angeles Kings, St. Louis Blues, 1979–80—1994–96

Most three-or-more goal games, career: 49, Wayne Gretzky, Edmonton Oilers, 1979–80—1994–96

Most scoring titles: 9, Wayne Gretzky, Edmonton Oilers, Los Angeles Kings, St. Louis Blues, 1981–87, 1990, 1991, 1994

Most Hart (MVP) trophies: 9, Wayne Gretzky, Edmonton Oilers, Los Angeles Kings, St. Louis Blues, 1980–87, 1989

Most goals, season: 92, Wayne Gretzky, Edmonton Oilers, 1981–82

Most assists, season: 163, Wayne Gretzky, Edmonton Oilers, 1985–86

Most points, season: 215, Wayne Gretzky, Edmonton Oilers, 1985–86

Most assists, game: 7, Wayne Gretzky, Edmonton Oilers, vs. Washington Capitals, Feb. 15, 1980; Wayne Gretzky, Edmonton Oilers, vs. Chicago Blackhawks, Dec. 11, 1985; Wayne Gretzky, Edmonton Oilers, vs. Quebec Nordiques, Feb. 14, 1986 (Ties Billy Taylor, Detroit Red Wings, vs. Chicago Blackhawks, March 16, 1947)

Wayne Gretzky was a King when he broke Gordie Howe's career goal-scoring record in 1994. *Bruce Bennett*

BOXING

Moore Knockouts

PHOENIX, Ariz., March 15, 1963—Former light heavyweight champion Archie Moore "unretired" tonight to pound professional wrestler Mike DiBiase for two rounds and 29 seconds before the fight was called, a technical knockout.

Boxing's knockout king, Archie Moore (left), won the light heavyweight title from Joey Maxim in 1952.   *Wide World*

The 50-year-old Moore, who has been boxing for 28 years, scored his first knockout in his first professional fight on Jan. 31, 1936, in Hot Springs, Ark., against the Poco Kid. Moore has more knockouts to his credit than any other man who stepped into the ring, but exactly how many—like his date of birth—is a point of contention. *Ring Magazine Encyclopedia,* which does not differentiate between knockouts and technical knockouts, credits Moore with 140.

Accuracy with numbers has never bothered Moore, who won his light heavyweight title from Joey Maxim in 1952. He claims Dec. 13, 1916, as his birthday, but his mother maintained Archibald Lee Wright was born in 1913 in Benoit, Miss.

Most knockouts, professional career: 140, Archie Moore, 1935–63

The Brockton Blockbuster

NEWTON, Iowa, Aug. 31, 1969—Rocky Marciano planned to celebrate his 46th birthday tomorrow at a party in Des Moines, Iowa. But the former world heavyweight champion was killed here with two others last night in a crash of a single-engine Cessna 172. He was en route from Chicago.

The Brockton Blockbuster won all 49 of his professional fights—43 by knockouts—before announcing his retirement in 1956. He came out of Brockton, Mass., where his father was a shoemaker, and he won the heavyweight title by knocking out Jersey Joe Walcott in 1952. During a three-and-a-half-year reign he defended his title six times, the last when he knocked out Archie Moore in 1955.

A rugged puncher, Marciano was counted among the best of the all-time heavyweights—in a class that included Jack Dempsey, Gene Tunney, and Joe Louis, the latter one of Marciano's knockout victims.

The only heavyweight champion without a loss or a draw over an entire career: Rocky Marciano, 49-for-49, March 17, 1947—Sept. 21, 1955

En route to the heavyweight crown, Rocky Marciano knocked out former champion Joe Louis.   *Wide World*

Ali's Triple

NEW ORLEANS, La., Sept. 15, 1978—It happened at the end of the seventh round. After landing two solid punches, 36-year-old Muhammad Ali ducked under a wild swing by heavyweight champion Leon Spinks as the bell sounded. Heading back to his corner, Ali went into his familiar dance, the Ali Shuffle. And the crowd of 70,000 at the Superdome cheered wildly. The old Ali was back.

Eight rounds later, it was all over. Ali, winner by unanimous decision, had captured the world championship for a record third time.

Muhammad Ali (left) regained the heavyweight title he'd lost to Leon Spinks by scoring a decision over Spinks in 1978. *Wide World*

He'd knocked out Sonny Liston in 1964 for his first title, he'd knocked out George Foreman in 1974 to win the title for the second time, and now he's lifted the crown from the 25-year-old Spinks, who had dethroned him seven months ago. Spinks wound up with the dubious distinction of having held the heavyweight title for the shortest time in history.

And once more Ali was the greatest.

Most times heavyweight champion: 3, Muhammad Ali, vs. Sonny Liston, KO7, Feb. 25, 1964; vs. George Foreman, KO8, Oct. 30, 1974; vs. Leon Spinks, W15, Sept. 15, 1978

Quickest KO

MARBELLA, Spain, Aug. 30, 1987—Welterweight champion Lloyd Honeyghan knocked out American challenger Gene Hatcher of Fort Worth, Tex., in 40 seconds of the first round to retain his World Boxing Council and International Boxing Federation titles.

The 27-year-old Jamaican-born Honeyghan used a series of quick combinations to put Hatcher on the ropes before finishing him off with a left hook to record the fastest knockout ever in a world title fight.

Honeyghan, who now resides in London, said his opening overhand right "was one of the best I've ever thrown."

The previous fastest knockout in a title fight was Sugar Ray Robinson's 52-second defense of his middleweight crown against Jose Barosa, Aug. 25, 1950.

Fastest knockout in a world championship fight: 40 seconds, Lloyd Honeyghan vs. Gene Hatcher, Aug. 30, 1987

Ring Methuselah

LAS VEGAS, Nev., Nov. 5, 1994—After nine rounds in which he looked his age, 45-year-old George Foreman connected with his target tonight at the MGM Grand Garden.

With an explosive right hand to the chin of 26-year-old Michael Moorer, the 250-pound Foreman knocked out the defending champion at 2:03 of the 10th round. Foreman thus became the oldest heavyweight champion in history.

The 222-pound Moorer had dominated the fight. All three judges had him ahead on their cards. But then came the knockout punch that made up for the 20 years of pain that Foreman had endured since he lost the heavyweight crown to Muhammad Ali in 1974.

The previous oldest champion was Jersey Joe Walcott, who won the heavyweight title at the age of 37 by defeating Ezzard Charles in 1952.

Oldest heavyweight champion: George Foreman, 45, 1994

It was one for the ages when 45-year-old George Foreman put away 26-year-old Michael Moorer in 1994. *Wide World*

COLLEGE
FOOTBALL

Mr. Inside and Mr. Outside

PHILADELPHIA, Pa., Nov. 30, 1946—The greatest era in Army football came to an end today as Mr. Inside and Mr. Outside played in their last collegiate game together. And it was almost a disaster. The Cadets, undefeated in three years (one scoreless tie with Notre Dame to blemish the slate), were saved by the clock. Navy, loser of seven straight after an opening-game victory, was in possession of the ball on the Army three-yard line, trailing 21–18 when the final gun sounded.

Army's Glenn Davis (right) set his rushing mark while being coached by Red Blaik and playing with Doc Blanchard (center).   *UPI*

The crowd of 100,000, including President Harry S. Truman, had watched the Cadets open up a 21–6 half-time lead with Mr. Inside, Doc Blanchard, scoring twice and Mr. Outside, Glenn Davis, picking up the other touchdown. The score by Davis, on a 13-yard run after a pitchout from Arnie Tucker, was the 59th of his varsity career, giving him 354 points. Before the day was out, Davis gained his 2,957th yard rushing for a record average of 8.26 yards per carry.

But nobody was thinking much about records in the second half of the game as Reeves Baysinger, Bill Hawkins, and Leon Bramlett sparked the Middies to what would have been the greatest upset in the Army-Navy series.

Highest rushing average, major college career (minimum 300 attempts): 8.26 yards per carry (358 rushes for 2,957 yards), Glenn Davis, Army, 1943–46

Beware the Hurricane

TULSA, Okla., Nov. 25, 1965—Tulsa's Howard Twilley caught two TD passes and kicked four extra points today to become the first receiver ever to win a national scoring title.

He wound up with 127 points as the Hurricanes achieved a come-from-behind 48–20 victory over Colorado State University.

It was a big day as well for Tulsa quarterback Bill Anderson, who uncorked fourth-quarter scoring passes of 60, 63, 51 and 13 yards. He had 37 completions in 57 attempts for 502 yards and five touchdowns.

Twilley wound up his career with an NCAA record 261 passes caught, among other marks.

Most passes caught, three-season career: 261, Howard Twilley, Tulsa, 1963–65

Most passes caught per game, season: 13.4, Howard Twilley, Tulsa, 1965

Most yards gained, pass receptions, season: 1,779, Howard Twilley, Tulsa, 1965

Most yards gained, pass receptions, per game, season: 177.9, Howard Twilley, Tulsa, 1965

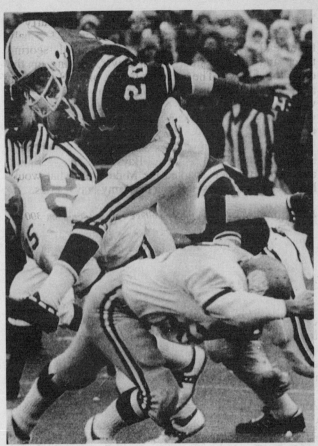

Nebraska's Johnny Rodgers tied two kick-return marks against Kansas State in 1972.   *UPI*

'Husker's Harvest

LINCOLN, Neb., Nov. 18, 1972—Nebraska's Johnny Rodgers opened the scoring today with a 52-yard run-back of a Kansas State punt for a touchdown and the Cornhuskers didn't stop scoring until they had whipped Kansas State, 59–7. The victory was the 100th in coach Bob Devaney's 11 years at Nebraska.

Rodgers also scored a touchdown in the second quarter, on an eight-yard run, before the game was turned over to the reserves. The touchdown on the punt return gave Rodgers a pair of NCAA records. It was the seventh time he had run back a punt for a TD, tying him with Oklahoma's Jack Mitchell in that department. Rodgers had also run back a kickoff for a touchdown, matching the eight TDs on kick returns by Colorado's Cliff Branch.

Most touchdowns on kick returns, career: 8, Johnny Rodgers, Nebraska, 1970–72 (seven punts, one kickoff) (Ties Cliff Branch, Colorado, 1970–71 [six punts, two kickoffs])

Most touchdowns on punt returns, major college career: 7, Johnny Rodgers, Nebraska, 1970–72 (Ties Jack Mitchell, Oklahoma, 1946–48)

Panther on the Prowl

PITTSBURGH, Pa., Nov. 26, 1976—Tony Dorsett, the No. 1 running back in the country, carried the ball for 224 yards and two touchdowns tonight in leading the No. 1-ranked Pitt Panthers to a 24–7 victory over Penn State. The Panthers thus completed their first unbeaten season since 1937, when they were also the top-ranked college football team.

The 5-foot 11-inch Dorsett, son of an Aliquippa, Pa., steel mill worker, became the first collegian to pass the 6,000-yard mark in rushing, as his 224 yards gave him a four-year total of 6,082. He also finished his campus career with a record 33 games in which he gained 100 or more yards.

Most yards gained rushing, career: 6,082, Tony Dorsett, Pittsburgh, 1973–76

Most games gaining 100 yards or more: 33, Tony Dorsett, Pittsburgh, 1973–76 (Ties Archie Griffin, Ohio State, 1972–75)

Pittsburgh's Tony Dorsett, scoring here against Notre Dame, was a record-smashing rusher in his four-year career.   *UPI*

McMahon Aloft

PROVO, Utah, Nov. 21, 1981—Brigham Young quarterback Jim McMahon completed 35 of 54 passes for 565 yards and four touchdowns today as the Cougars romped over the University of Utah, 56–28.

With the Western Athletic Conference title and a Holiday Bowl bid awaiting the winner of this traditional intrastate clash, Utah jumped off to an early 10–7 lead before McMahon threw an eight-yard scoring strike to Gordon Hudson to give BYU a lead it never relinquished. The 6-foot 1-inch, 180-pound McMahon also hit on touchdown passes of 6, 27 and 37 yards in front of a record crowd of 47,163.

McMahon, who was born in Jersey City, N.J., and

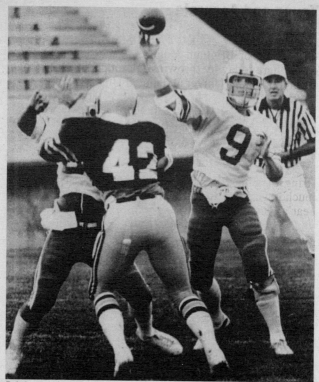

Brigham Young's Jim McMahon rewrote many collegiate passing
marks. *Wide World*

grew up in California, ended his final regular-season
game owning or sharing 57 NCAA records.

Most points responsible for per game (passing, scoring) two consecutive seasons: 22.8 (502 points in 22 games), Jim McMahon, Brigham Young, 1980–81

Young and Accurate

PROVO, Utah, Nov. 19, 1983—Steve Young, a direct descendant of Brigham Young, closed out his college career here today by throwing six touchdown passes as Brigham Young University routed Utah, 55–7.

Passing with remarkable accuracy, the lefthanded Young connected on 22 of 25 passes for 268 yards, giving him a record completion average for the season of 71.3 percent as he clicked on 306 passes in 429 attempts.

Utilizing five different receivers on his scoring throws, the 6-foot 2-inch Young also extended his string of games in which he has thrown at least one touchdown pass to a record 22, dating back to last year's season opener.

Highest percentage of passes completed, season: 71.3 percent, Steve Young, Brigham Young, 1983 (306 of 429)

Run 'em Cowboy

TOKYO, Japan, Dec. 4, 1988—Oklahoma State's Barry Sanders showed why he won the Heisman Trophy just a few hours ago as he scored four times and rushed for a season-high 332 yards in leading the Cowboys to a 45–42 victory over Texas Tech at the Tokyo Dome.

As happy as he was with the effort on this Sunday afternoon, Sanders was downright unhappy early this morning. A man who shuns ceremony and particularly dislikes distractions on the day of a game, Sanders reluctantly showed up at a local television studio for a 7:50 A.M. television hookup in conjunction with the Heisman award from New York, where it was 5:50 P.M. Saturday afternoon.

As a 5-foot 8-inch, 175-pound senior at North High in Wichita, Kan., Sanders was overlooked by many college recruiters. Even at Oklahoma State, he was used mainly as a kick-returner and as backfield starter to give Thurman Thomas an occasional rest. Moving up to starter this season, all Sanders did was rush for 238.9 yards a game, break the touchdown record (shared by Penn State's Lydell Mitchell and Nebraska's Mike Rozier) by 60 points, and amass 3,250 all-purpose yards rushing, receiving, and returning kicks.

Most yards rushing, season: 2,628, Barry Sanders, Oklahoma State, 1988

Most yards gained rushing per game, season: 238.9, Barry Sanders, Oklahoma State, 1988

Most touchdowns rushing, season: 37, Barry Sanders, Oklahoma State, 1988

Most touchdowns, season: 39, Barry Sanders, Oklahoma State, 1988

Most all-purpose yards gained, season: 3,250, Barry Sanders, Oklahoma State, 1988

Most all-purpose yards gained per game, season: 295.5, Barry Sanders, Oklahoma State, 1988

Rocket Returns

ANN ARBOR, Mich., Sept. 16, 1989—Notre Dame's Raghib Ismail, known as the Rocket, returned two second-half kickoffs for touchdowns to lead the Fighting Irish to a 24–19 victory today over Michigan before a rain-dampened crowd of 105,912.

Notre Dame strengthened its position as the top-ranked team in the country as it extended its winning streak to 14 games and a 2–0 record this season.

With Notre Dame leading, 7–6, at halftime, the 5-foot 10-inch Ismail, a sophomore from Wilkes-Barre, Pa., took the opening kickoff of the second half and returned it 88 yards for a score. It was the first time in 32 years that anyone had returned a kickoff for a TD against the Wolverines.

Then, early in the fourth quarter, after Michigan had closed to within five points at 17–12 on a five-yard pass from Elvis Grbac to tight end Derrick Walker, Ismail gathered in the ensuing kickoff on his own eight-yard line and zigzagged 92 yards for another touchdown.

As a freshman last year, Ismail had returned two kickoffs for touchdowns in a 43-point blowout over Rice. Today's returns against the much tougher Wolverines were much more significant, but Ismail played down his effort.

"The only thing I have to do," he said after today's game, "is to make one person miss. When everyone takes care of their blocking assignments and I make one person miss, we do pretty well."

Most times returned kickoffs for two touchdowns in one game, career: 2, Raghib "Rocket" Ismail, Notre Dame, vs. Rice, Nov. 5, 1988, and vs. Michigan, Sept. 16, 1989

Go Johnny Go

KINGSVILLE, Tex., Nov. 11, 1989—Texas A&I's Johnny Bailey, averaging more than 158 yards a game rushing this season, didn't get much of a chance to show what he could do this afternoon as the Javelinas scored early and often in routing Angelo State, 42–3, to capture the Lone Star Conference championship and the No. 1 seed in the NCAA Division II playoffs.

The victory improved Texas A&I's record to 10–0 for the season. Angelo State finished 9–2, but still managed to gain a berth in the playoffs.

The lopsided score prompted A&I coach Ron Harms to rest Bailey early, and as a result he turned in the worst performance of his career—statistically speaking. Bailey gained just 56 yards in 15 carries, caught two passes for 20 yards and scored one touchdown.

Still, the 5-foot 9-inch Houston native finished his collegiate career with 6,320 yards rushing, breaking the all-division NCAA mark set by Tony Dorsett at Pitt from 1973 to 1976. Bailey's 7.14-yards-per-carry and 162.1-yards-per-game rushing averages are the highest in any division for players with at least 5,000 career rushing yards.

In addition, Bailey set a collegiate record of 7,803 all-purpose yards (rushing, receiving and returns), as did his average of 200.1 all-purpose yards per game. In all, Bailey finished with more than 100 NCAA, Lone Star Conference and Texas A&I school records.

Most yards gained rushing, career, all divisions: 6,320, Johnny Bailey, Texas A&I, 1986–89

Hustling Hoosier

CHAMPAIGN, Ill., Nov. 18, 1989—Indiana's Anthony Thompson carried the ball 38 times for 189 yards, including a 20-yard touchdown run, but Illinois, led by Jeff George's five TD passes, prevailed for a 41–28 Big Ten victory today.

Thompson, who set an NCAA single-game rushing record with 377 yards on 52 carries against Wisconsin last week, now has scored 394 points in his career on 65 touchdowns and four extra points. His point total is one more than kicker Derek Schmidt compiled on 73 field goals and 174 PATs at Florida State, 1984–1987.

Today's third-quarter score gave Thompson 64 rushing touchdowns, extending his major college career record in that category. The previous mark had been 56, set by Oklahoma's Steve Owens, 1967–69.

Most points scored, career, I-A: 394, Anthony Thompson, Indiana, 1986–89

Most touchdowns rushing, career, I-A: 64, Anthony Thompson, Indiana, 1986–89

Toast of Champaign

CHAMPAIGN, Ill., Sept. 22, 1990—Illinois fullback Howard Griffith's eight touchdowns broke some of the oldest records in the book as 15th-ranked Illinois walloped Southern Illinois, 56–21, today in Memorial Stadium.

The 5-foot 11-inch, 218-pound senior scored on a five-yard run early in the first quarter after Division

I-AA Southern Illinois had jumped out to an early lead. Griffith then scored on runs of 51 yards, 7 yards, and 41 yards in the second quarter to help the Illini to a 28–21 lead at halftime.

The five TDs tied the Illinois school record set by The Galloping Ghost, Red Grange, on the day Memorial Stadium was dedicated in 1924.

Griffith took sole possession of that record with a five-yard jaunt early in the third quarter. Touchdown No. 6 came minutes later on an 18-yard run, followed quickly by another five-yard scoring romp that gave him seven TDs, tying him for the all-time collegiate record set by Mississippi's Arnold "Showboat" Boykin against Mississippi State in 1951.

Resting on the sidelines, Griffith later recalled, "I told Coach [John] Mackovic that it was up to him if he wanted to go for the record. I'm just happy to be in the company of names like that."

Mackovic sent him back late in the third quarter and Griffith scored TD No. 8 on a three-yard plunge, giving him not only the touchdown record, but also the single-game scoring record of 48 points. The previous mark of 43 was set by Jim Brown of Syracuse, who scored six touchdowns and seven extra points against Colgate in 1956.

Most touchdowns scored, major college game: 8, Howard Griffith, Illinois, vs. Southern Illinois, Sept. 22, 1990
Most points, major college game: 48, Howard Griffith, Illinois, vs. Southern Illinois, Sept. 22, 1990

A Cougar's Collection

TOKYO, Japan, Dec. 2, 1990—Playing in the Mirage Bowl, Houston quarterback David Klingler closed out his junior year in spectacular fashion, passing for a record 716 yards as the Cougars whipped Arizona State, 62–45.

In setting a raft of single-game and one-season records, Klingler connected on 41 of 70 passes, including seven scoring strikes. He ended the season with 5,140 passing yards, an NCAA record that lasted only a matter of hours until Brigham Young's Heisman Trophy winner Ty Detmer finished his season in a game against Hawaii.

Most total offense yards, game: 732, David Klingler, Houston, Dec. 2, 1990

Most passing yards, game: 716, David Klingler, Houston, Dec. 2, 1990

Most passes attempted, season: 643, David Klingler, Houston, 1990

Most passes completed, season: 374, David Klingler, Houston, 1990

Most yards per game passing, season: 467.3, David Klingler, Houston, 1990

Ty Terrific

PROVO, Utah, Nov. 23, 1991—In the final regular-season game of a record-smashing career, Brigham Young's Ty Detmer fired five touchdown passes today in a 48–17 trouncing of Utah.

The 6-foot, 175-pound four-year quarterback even added a touchdown rushing as he extended his NCAA TD pass mark to 121. He hit on 18 of 29 passes for 378 yards and one of his TD aerials was a 97-yard play with receiver Eric Drage.

Earlier this season, last year's Heisman Trophy winner played a major role in the 52–52 stalemate with San Diego State, the highest-scoring tie game in NCAA history. His other records include most yards passing in a season and 24 consecutive games passing for 300 yards in his first three years.

Most touchdown passes, career: 121, Ty Detmer, Brigham Young, 1988–91

Most yards gained passing, season: 5,188, Ty Detmer, Brigham Young, 1990

Most consecutive games passing for 300 yards: 24, Ty Detmer, Brigham Young, Sept. 2, 1989–Nov. 23, 1991

Highest-scoring tie game in NCAA history: 52–52, Brigham Young vs. San Diego State, Nov. 16, 1991

Brigham Young's Ty Detmer followed up his Heisman Trophy
season with record highs in 1991.   *Wide World*

Air McNair

JACKSON, Miss., Nov. 19, 1994—Heisman Trophy
candidate Steve McNair threw for 533 yards and five
touchdowns to lead Alcorn State to a 52–34 victory today over Jackson State before a crowd of 62,512 at
Mississippi Veterans Memorial Stadium.

McNair, who owns a slew of NCAA Division I-AA
and all-division records, completed 29 of 54 passes. He
also rushed for 31 yards to account for 564 yards of total offense. In leading the Braves to an 8–2–1 record
and a playoff berth, McNair completed 304 of 530

passes for 4,863 yards and 44 TDs. In addition, he rushed for 936 yards and nine TDs.

He ends his career as the all-time collegiate leader in total offense with 16,823 yards for an average of 400.5 yards per game, also a record. The 527.2 yards per game he averaged this year is a single-season all-division record. In addition, he has four of the 10-highest single-game total offense performances in the NCAA record book.

Most total offense yards, career: 16,823, Steve McNair, Alcorn State, 1991–94

Highest total offense average, career: 400.5 yards per game, Steve McNair, Alcorn State, 1991–94

Most offensive plays, career: 2,055, Steve McNair, Alcorn State, 1991–94

Most yards passing per game, career: 345.1, Steve McNair, Alcorn State, 1991–94

Most total offense yards, season: 5,799, Steve McNair, Alcorn State, 1994

Highest total offense average, season: 527.2 yards per game, Steve McNair, Alcorn State, 1994

Alcorn State's Steve McNair has more than a few lines in the NCAA record book.   *Wide World*

COLLEGE
BASKETBALL

Backboard Dukes

NEW YORK, March 14, 1953—No. 1-seeded Seton Hall had little trouble with St. John's University tonight as 7-foot Walter Dukes led the Pirates to a 58–46 victory and the National Invitation Tournament championship before a crowd of 18,496, the largest ever to watch a collegiate game in Madison Square Garden.

Seton Hall's Walter Dukes collected rebounds all season and the MVP award for his play in the NIT. *UPI*

Dukes, the first black to win unanimous All-American honors, scored 21 points and pulled down 20 rebounds en route to winning the tournament MVP trophy. The 20 rebounds brought his total for the season to 734, an all-time record. Dukes is a native of Rochester, N.Y., where he was spotted working in his mother's dry cleaning store by Bob Davies of the Rochester Royals, a former Seton Hall star. Davies persuaded Dukes to attend Seton Hall, located in South Orange, N.J.

Tonight's championship was accomplished with the same ease that the Pirates displayed in compiling a 28–2 regular-season record before sweeping Niagara, Manhattan, and St. John's in the NIT. Little Richie Regan was the floor leader, racking up seven assists on feeds to Dukes and scoring 13 points.

Most rebounds, major college season: 734, Walter Dukes, Seton Hall, 1952–53

The Paladins' Gun

GREENVILLE, S.C., Feb. 13, 1954—Paladin Frank Selvy used his gun often and well tonight as he shot the basketball through the hoop for a record 100 points in leading Furman to a 149–95 rout of little Newberry College.

The 6-foot 3-inch Selvy put on the show for his parents, who were visiting with friends from his hometown of Corbin, Ky. The Paladin senior, the leading scorer in the nation, started out with 24 points in the first quarter and added another 13 in the second. By the end of the third period, he had 62 and his teammates began to feed him the ball every time the Paladins were on offense.

By the middle of the fourth quarter he had broken the NCAA record of 73 points in one game, set by Temple's Bill Mlkvy in 1951. Selvy was also lucky that Newberry didn't try to stall or slow the game down in order to frustrate his shooting for the record. By the time the final gun sounded, Selvy had pumped in 38

points in the period to give him a nice round figure—
100 points.

Most points, major college game: 100, Frank Selvy, Furman, vs.
Newberry, Feb. 13, 1954

Furman's Frank Selvy gunned his way to the century mark.   *UPI*

Carr's Finer Points

DAYTON, Ohio, March 7, 1970—Hitting from long range as well as on driving layups, Austin Carr scored a record 61 points tonight in leading Notre Dame to a 112–82 rout of Ohio University in the opening round of the NCAA Mideast Regional basketball tournament.

The 6-foot 3-inch Carr, a product of Mackin High School in Washington, D.C., broke the tournament record of 58 points set by Princeton's Bill Bradley in 1965. Carr hit on 25 of 44 field goal attempts and 11 of 14 foul shots.

Most points, NCAA tournament, game: 61, Austin Carr, Notre Dame, vs. Ohio University, March 7, 1970

Notre Dame's Austin Carr hit 61 points for an NCAA tournament record.   *UPI*

Pistol's Parting Shots

NEW YORK, March 19, 1970—"Pistol Pete" Maravich, the highest scorer in major college history, was held to 20 points in the final game of his college career tonight as Marquette whipped Louisiana State, 101–79, to advance to the finals of the National Invitation Tournament at Madison Square Garden.

Maravich was hampered by an ankle injury sustained in a quarterfinal-round victory over Oklahoma in which he pumped in 37 points. Tonight, not only did the

"Pistol Pete" Maravich ended his college career in the NIT.   *UPI*

Warriors double-team him, but they also choked off the passing lanes so Maravich could not feed his teammates with passes that are often as dazzling and unorthodox as his shots. The ankle injury will keep Pete out of tomorrow afternoon's consolation game against Jacksonville.

Maravich, who has played his entire varsity career under the coaching of his father, Press, owns these collegiate records:

Most points, major college, season: 1,381, Pete Maravich, LSU, 1969–70

Highest scoring average, major college, season: 44.5 points per game, Pete Maravich, LSU, 1969–70

Most field goals attempted, major college, season: 1,168, Pete Maravich, LSU, 1969–70

Most field goals made, major college, season: 522, Pete Maravich, LSU, 1969–70

Most points, major college, career: 3,667, Pete Maravich, LSU, 1967–68 to 1969–70

Highest scoring average, major college, career: 44.2 points per game Pete Maravich, LSU, 1967–68 to 1969–70

Most field goals attempted, major college, career: 3,166, Pete Maravich, LSU, 1967–68 to 1969–70

Most field goals made, major college, career: 1,387, Pete Maravich, LSU, 1967–68 to 1969–70

Bruin Power

SOUTH BEND, Ind., Jan. 19, 1974—A short jump shot by Dwight Clay with 29 seconds left to play provided a 71–70 victory for Notre Dame today as the Fighting Irish snapped UCLA's winning streak at 88, the longest in college basketball history. UCLA had made Iowa its 88th consecutive victim in a game two nights ago at the Chicago Stadium, winning easily, 68–44.

The last time the Bruins had lost a game was on this same court three years ago—Jan. 23, 1971—when Austin Carr's 46 points led Notre Dame to victory. Since that time, UCLA won its fifth, sixth, and seventh consecutive NCAA championships.

UCLA's record streak started Jan. 30, 1971, with a 74–61 victory over the University of California at Santa

Notre Dame's Dwight Clay led the upset that ended UCLA's 88-game winning streak.   *UPI*

Barbara. The Bruins depended then on players like Curtis Rowe, Sidney Wicks, Steve Patterson, and Henry Bibby. The next three years the mainstays were Bill Walton and Keith Wilkes. Today was the first time in their varsity careers that Walton and Wilkes were on the losing side.

The game between UCLA and Notre Dame was billed as a showdown between the teams' two centers, 6-foot 11-inch Walton and 6-foot 9-inch John Shumate of ND. Each scored 24 points, rebounded well, and played tough defense. The difference was the ball-handling and shooting of Notre Dame's 6-foot 4-inch Gary Brokaw, who scored 25 points, led a burst in the last three minutes in which the Irish outscored UCLA 12–0, and found Clay open for the final score of the game.

Most consecutive victories: 88, UCLA, Jan. 30, 1971, to Jan. 17, 1974

Hoosiers on a Roll

PHILADELPHIA, Pa., March 29, 1976—Undefeated Indiana, led by Scott May, Quinn Buckner and Kent Benson, overcame a 35–29 halftime deficit tonight to rout Michigan, 86–68, for the NCAA championship and its 32nd victory.

Bobby Knight's Hoosiers, who had ousted defending champion UCLA in the semifinals, prevailed despite the loss of defensive standout Bobby Wilkerson, who was literally knocked out by an errant elbow in the first half. May and Benson paced the winners with 26 and 25 points, respectively.

Indiana became the seventh team in history to complete the regular season and the NCAA Tournament without a setback. Thus the Hoosiers tied the NCAA mark for most victories in an undefeated season, set by North Carolina in 1957 when it defeated Wilt Chamberlain-led Kansas, 54–53, in triple overtime.

Most victories, undefeated, season: 32, Indiana, 1975–76 (Ties North Carolina, 1956–57)

Bruce Morris of Marshall University sank the longest shot.

Marshall/SPS

Herculean Heave

HUNTINGTON, W. Va., Feb. 7, 1985—Desperation shots at the end of a half or game are commonplace in basketball, but Bruce Morris of Marshall University did the uncommon tonight. He sank a shot from 92 feet, 5¼ inches away from the basket.

With just three seconds remaining in the first half of a game against Appalachian State, the 6-foot 4-inch Morris picked up a blocked shot at the baseline. He turned and, heaving the ball like a baseball, sent it swishing through the net at the other end of the court. Marshall went on to win the game, 93–82.

Morris, a native of Deerfield, Ill., described how it happened afterward. "The ball just fell straight down in my arms, and I turned and saw the clock and just let it go. When I saw it going, I knew it would hit something or be pretty close because it looked kind of accurate."

As the low-trajectory shot slipped through the hoop, he said, "I looked at the ref to see if it had counted, and it did."

Longest field goal: 92 feet, 5¹/₄ inches, Bruce Morris, Marshall, vs. Appalachian State, Feb. 7, 1985

Three-Point Landing

INDIANAPOLIS, Ind., Feb. 27, 1987—Darrin Fitzgerald, a 5-foot 8-inch, 150-pound senior, wound up his career tonight with three NCAA records for three-point goals.

The Butler University long-distance ace registered five three-pointers among his 34 points, but Xavier beat the Bulldogs, 104–98. Marking the first year of the three-point goal in NCAA play, Fitzgerald had a season mark of 158 three-pointers in 362 attempts.

Earlier in the season, Fitzgerald scored 12 three-pointers against Detroit to tie the record set by Niagara's Gary Bossert against Siena. Fitzgerald's 5.6 three-point-goal average per game is also a record.

Most three-point field goals, season: 158 (362 attempts), Darrin Fitzgerald, Butler, 1986–87
Most three-point field-goal attempts, season: 362, Darrin Fitzgerald, Butler, 1986–87
Highest three-point-goals-per-game average, season: 5.6 (158 in 28 games), Darrin Fitzgerald, Butler, 1986–87

Navy's David Robinson won honors as the best man on the block.
U.S. Naval Academy/SPS

Naval Blockade

CHARLOTTE, N.C., March 12, 1987—David Robinson said farewell tonight as the greatest player in Navy history. A one-man fleet, the 7-foot 1-inch All-American center scored 50 points as Michigan ousted the Midshipmen, 97–85, in the first round of the NCAA playoffs.

Thus ended a brilliant four-year career in which

Robinson scored 2,669 points and had a .613 shooting percentage. But it was his shot-blocking that landed him in the NCAA record book. As a junior in 1985–86, Robinson blocked 14 shots against North Carolina–Wilmington, giving him 207 blocked shots for the season, a 5.9 average. All are NCAA records. And so is his 5.2 career average.

Most blocked shots, game: 14—David Robinson, Navy, vs. North Carolina–Wilmington, Jan. 4, 1986
Most blocked shots, season: 207—David Robinson, Navy, 1985–86
Highest average per game, blocked shots, season: 5.9, David Robinson, 1985–86 (207 in 35 games)
Highest average per game, blocked shots, career: 5.2, David Robinson, 1986–87
(Note: Career blocked-shot averages were not kept as official NCAA stats until 1986–87.)

Pointing the Way

LOS ANGELES, Cal., Jan. 5, 1991—In a scoring circus pairing Loyola Marymount and U.S. International tonight, Kevin Bradshaw registered 72 points to set a record for NCAA Division I competition.

Bradshaw, a 6-foot 6-inch, 190-pound U.S. International senior, threw up 29 shots, including 22 three-pointers. He connected on 23 shots, including seven threes, and he clicked on 19 of 23 foul shots.

It all was to no avail as Loyola Marymount won, 186–140, but Bradshaw's harvest broke the 20-year record of 69 points set by Louisiana State's Pete Maravich against Alabama in 1970. At the same time Loyola Marymount's 186 points broke its own mark of 181 points set a year ago against, of all teams, U.S. International.

Most points, vs. Division I opponent: 72, Kevin Bradshaw, U.S. International, vs. Loyola Marymount, Jan. 5, 1991
Most points, one team: 186, Loyola Marymount, vs. U.S. International (140), Jan. 5, 1991

Double-Figure Jayhawk

LAWRENCE, Kans., March 7, 1988—In his final appearance at Allen Field House tonight, All-American Danny Manning hit on 14 of 20 shots from the field and three of four free throws to score 31 points and lead Kansas past Oklahoma State, 75–57.

The emotionally charged crowd threw roses on the court, blew kisses toward Manning, and cheered their hero. On hand to see the display were Manning's mother, Darnelle, and father, Ed, an assistant to Jayhawks coach Larry Brown. They saw their son score in double figures for a record 132nd time in his collegiate career.

After the game, the 6-foot 10-inch forward said, "It's bittersweet—bad that I have to leave my teammates and KU, but good because I'm ready to move on and face new challenges."

Most games scoring double figures, career: 132, Danny Manning, Kansas, 1984–88

On the Block

LANDOVER, Md., March 7, 1992—With time running out, Georgetown center Alonzo Mourning batted away a shot by Pittsburgh's Chris McNeal for his eighth and final block of the game as the Hoyas beat the Panthers, 67–57, at the Capital Centre today.

Mourning, who was forced to sit out nearly a quarter of the game with foul trouble, was the game's high scorer with 20 points. He also pulled down 11 rebounds in the final game of a season that saw Georgetown finish in a three-way tie with Seton Hall and St. John's for first place in the Big East standings.

The eight blocked shots increased Mourning's NCAA-record career total to 453 in 120 games.

Most blocked shots, career: 453, Alonzo Mourning, Georgetown, 1989–92

Georgetown's Alonzo Mourning blocked the most shots in NCAA history.

Georgetown/SPS

Dishing It Out

CHAPEL HILL, N.C., March 7, 1993—Playing without the injured Grant Hill, Duke was no match for North Carolina this afternoon as the No. 1-ranked Tar Heels polished off the sixth-ranked Blue Devils, 83–69, in the season-ender for both teams.

Duke's Bobby Hurley emerged as the all-time assists leader.

Wide World

With Hill sitting on the bench in street clothes, Duke was harassed into taking poor shoots and connected on just 22 of 62 field-goal attempts. Blue Devil senior guard Bobby Hurley still managed to come up with a half-dozen assists to extend his NCAA career-record total to 1,076 in 140 games.

Most assists, career: 1,076, Bobby Hurley, Duke, 1990–93

Swoopes' Hoops

ATLANTA, Ga., April 4, 1993—Ohio State hit two three-point field goals in the final 12 seconds, but it was too little too late today as Sheryl Swoopes scored 47 points in leading Texas Tech to an 84–82 victory over the Buckeyes to win the NCAA Division I women's basketball championship.

The 6-foot Swoopes made her first seven shots of the game and 16 of 24 overall, including four three-pointers. She also was perfect from the free-throw line, going 11-for-11. Her 47 points are the most ever scored in an NCAA championship game, men's or women's.

The performance capped a major assault on the record book as Swoopes set 10 records, including most points in the women's tournament with 177 and averaging 35.4 points per game.

Most points, national championship game: 47, Sheryl Swoopes, Texas Tech, April 4, 1993

Most points, postseason tournament: 177, Sheryl Swoopes, Texas Tech, 1993

Most field goals, postseason tournament: 56, Sheryl Swoopes, Texas Tech, 1993

Most free throws, postseason tournament: 57, Sheryl Swoopes, Texas Tech, 1993

Highest free throw percentage, postseason tournament (minimum 20 attempts): 93.4%, Sheryl Swoopes, Texas Tech, 1993 (57 of 61)

Texas Tech's Sheryl Swoopes highlighted the NCAA Division I
championships with a 47-point barrage.   *Ian Halperin*

TRACK AND FIELD

Doing What He Oerter

MEXICO CITY, Mexico, Oct. 15, 1968—As a 20-year-old sophomore at Kansas University, Al Oerter made it to Australia, where he won the gold medal with a record 184-foot 11-inch toss of the discus at the 1956 Olympic Games in Melbourne.

In 1960, the 6-foot, 275-pound Oerter won the gold again at the Olympics in Rome with a record 194–2. Despite a rib injury and neck ailment, he made it three Olympic golds in a row with another record toss of 200–1 at Tokyo in 1964.

Today, at the age of 32, he did it again at the Olympics with a record 212–6 and his fourth straight gold medal. Oerter thus became the only athlete to have won four golds in the same event at separate Games.

Four gold medals in one event, separate Olympic Games: Al Oerter,
U.S., discus, 1956, 1960, 1964, 1968

California Gold Rush

LOS ANGELES, Cal., Aug. 11, 1984—Running the anchor leg of the 4 × 100-meter relay, Carl Lewis took the baton with a three-meter lead and stretched it into a seven-meter margin at the finish line as he earned his fourth gold medal of the Olympic Games today.

The 23-year-old Lewis had already won gold medals by taking the 100-meter dash in 9.99 seconds, the

Al Oerter wins the first of his four gold medals at the 1956 Olympics in Melbourne, Australia.

UPI

200-meters in Olympic record time of 19.80 seconds, and the long jump with a leap of 8.54 meters, or 28 feet, 1/4 inch. The relay quartet of Sam Graddy, Ron Brown, Calvin Smith, and Lewis produced the only track-and-field world record of the Los Angeles Olympics, with a time of 37.83 seconds.

Carl Lewis nears the finish in the 200-meter run, one of his four gold-medal events at the 1984 Olympics in Los Angeles.   *Wide World*

Lewis's four track-and-field gold medals matched the achievement of Jesse Owens, who earned them in the same four events as Lewis, in the 1936 Games held in Berlin.

Born in Birmingham, Ala., raised in Willingboro, N.J., and currently a resident of Houston, Tex., where he attended the University of Houston, Lewis recalled the one time he had met Owens. "Jesse Owens is still the same to me—a legend," Lewis said after winning his fourth medal. "Without the inspiration he gave me, I wouldn't be here today."

Most gold medals won, track and field, one Olympics: 4, Carl Lewis, Los Angeles, 1984 (Ties Jesse Owens, U.S., Berlin, 1936)

About Time

ZURICH, Switzerland, Aug. 7, 1988—Harry Lee "Butch" Reynolds, Jr., a native Ohioan who had run for Ohio State, knew all about the 43.8-second world record set by Lee Evans of the United States in the 400-meter dash at the 1968 Olympic Games in Mexico City.

The record had stood for nearly 20 years, the oldest running mark, and Butch was determined to break it. He did so today in the Weltklasse Grand Prix with a 43.29 clocking. Two of his countrymen, Danny Everett and Steve Lewis, were second and third at 44.20 and 44.26.

World record, 400 meters: 43.29, Harry Lee "Butch" Reynolds, Aug. 7, 1988

The Longest Leap

TOKYO, Japan, Aug. 30, 1991—Bob Beamon's remarkable long-jump record stood for 23 years—from the day he leaped 29 feet, 2½ inches at the Mexico City Olympic Games in 1968.

Today, the record came tumbling down when 27-year-old Mike Powell, who was born in Philadelphia, jumped 29 feet, 4½ inches in the world championships.

Native New Yorker Beamon's gold-medal feat had

Mike Powell cleared a long-standing mark in the long jump in 1991.
Wide World

shattered the mark of 27 feet, 4³/₄ inches shared by America's Ralph Boston (1965) and Russia's Igor Ter-Ovanesyan (1967).

World record, long jump: 29 feet, 4¹/₂ inches, Mike Powell, Aug. 30, 1991

Oh So High

SALAMANCA, Spain, July 27, 1993—Cuba's Javier Sotomayor, breaking the eight-foot barrier in the high jump, raised the world record to 8 feet, ¹/₂ inch today at the Salamanca Invitational track meet.

He cleared the height on his second attempt and though the crossbar wobbled on the standards, it stayed up. Sotomayor broke his own record of an even eight feet set four years ago in San Juan, Puerto Rico.

After today's effort, he said, "I wanted to set the record here because it's a small city in which I feel like I'm in Cuba. The people recognize me in the street and ask me how I'm doing, the children surround me, and I find myself in a good mental state."

World record, high jump: 8 feet, ¹/₂ inch, Javier Sotomayor, July 27, 1993

Morceli's Mile

RIETI, Italy, Sept. 5, 1993—Algerian Noureddine Morceli clipped 1.93 seconds off the world record for the mile, lowering the time to 3:44.39 at the Rieti Invitational track and field meet here today.

In lowering the record by the largest margin in 28 years, the 23-year-old Morceli shattered the mark of 3:46.32 set by Steve Cram of Britain in Oslo, Norway, on July 25, 1985.

Morceli, who attended Riverside Community College in California, finished a disappointing seventh in the 1,500-meter event at last year's Olympic Games in Barcelona. He redeemed himself after that, however, by running a world record time of 3:28.86 in the 1,500

Cuba's Javier Sotomayor became the first 8-foot man in the high jump in 1993. *Wide World*

meters at last year's Rieti Invitational. He has been un-beaten in both the 1,500 meters and mile events so far this year.

World record, mile: 3:44.39, Noureddine Morceli, Sept. 5, 1993
World record, 1,500 meters: 3:28.86, Noureddine Morceli, Sept. 6, 1992

Up and Over Again and Again

SESTRIERE, Italy, July 31, 1994—Taking advantage of the mile-and-a-quarter-high altitude here in the Italian Alps, Sergei Bubka raised the world record in the pole vault for the 35th time in his career, lifting the standard to 20 feet, 1³/₄ inches. This broke his old mark of 20 feet 1¹/₄ inches set two years ago in Tokyo.

A native of the Ukraine, Bubka was able to overcome the swirling, gusty winds that had frustrated other athletes today. "The wind was good, blowing in the proper direction. The track was perfect, and the altitude possibly helped," he said.

In explaining how he has been able to break the world record so many times, usually by a fraction of an inch each time, Bubka has said that a prime incentive is the bonus money meet promoters pay him for setting a record.

World record, pole vault: 20 feet, 1³/₄ inches, 1994, Sergei Bubka, July 31, 1994

Going Like 60

GOTEBERG, Sweden, Aug. 7, 1995—On his first attempt in the triple jump in the world track and field championships at Ullevi Stadium here today, 29-year-old Jonathan Edwards of Britain hopped, stepped and jumped 59 feet 7 inches to break his month-old world record of 59 feet.

On his second attempt, Edwards became the first man to triple-jump further than 60 feet, extending his best-in-the-world distance to 60 feet ¹/₄ inch.

A physics graduate whose father is a vicar in the Church of England, Edwards relaxed between attempts by playing chess. But he was a nervous wreck after he jumped as he waited for the official distances to be posted, chewing his knuckles, sucking air in and out, and licking his lips.

When the record numbers went up, Edwards said, "It's a humbling thing. I knew if I jumped well I was capable of winning and breaking the world record, but I almost didn't dare believe it."

World record, triple jump: 60 feet, ¹/₄ inch, Jonathan Edwards, Aug. 7, 1995

Sergei Bubka continued his assault on the pole vault record in 1994. *Wide World*

GOLF

"The Haig"

DALLAS, Texas, Nov. 5, 1927—Walter Hagen rallied from three holes behind today to defeat Joe Turnesa, one up, and win his fourth consecutive Professional Golfers Association championship. It was the fifth time the dark-eyed, slick-haired Hagen, known as "The Haig," has won the event.

Turnesa did not give up easily, going one up on the first nine holes this morning, picking up another on

Walter Hagen won the most consecutive PGA championships. *UPI*

the back nine, and going three up on the first hole of the afternoon round. Hagen, a native of Rochester, N.Y., came on strong after that, however, and pecked away at the lead until he went one up on the 13th hole. The two men played even the rest of the way.

Hagen won his first PGA in 1921. Two years later he was beaten by Gene Sarazen in a memorable contest at the Pelham Country Club in New York. Since then, The Haig has won them all, a record four in a row.

Most consecutive PGA championships: 4, Walter Hagen, 1924–27

Link to Greatness

ARDMORE, Pa., Sept. 27, 1930—The crowd around the 11th green at the Merion Cricket Club hushed as Bobby Jones addressed the ball. Jones—trying to become the only man ever to complete a golfing "grand slam"—stood about 20 feet from the cup. He tapped the ball gently. It rolled toward the cup, but slowed too quickly. It did not have the legs.

The 28-year-old Southern gentleman from Atlanta was not really trying to make the putt, though. He wanted a good shot, but more importantly, he wanted to put the pressure on his championship-round opponent, Gene Homans.

In May, Jones had won the British Amateur title at St. Andrews; in June he took the British Open at Hoylake and the U.S. Open at Interlachen, near Minneapolis. Now the U.S. Amateur was at stake. Jones had led all scorers in the 36-hole qualifying round of medal play and had breezed through the opening rounds of match play in the tourney. In today's 36-hole championship round, on the 29th hole, Jones was eight strokes ahead of Homans with eight holes left to play.

The approach putt by Jones had set up a do-or-die situation for Homans. Both men reached the green in two strokes. Jones' putt was his third shot. Homans had to sink a difficult putt or lose, 8 and 7. Homans' shot never got close. Before the ball had stopped rolling,

Homans was crossing the green to shake the hand of the only man ever to complete a golfing grand slam.

Most golf grand slams: 1, Robert Tyre Jones, Jr., 1930

Bobby Jones completes golf's only grand slam in the U.S. Amateur Championship at Ardmore, Pa., in 1930. *UPI*

Queen of Swing

HOPKINS, Minn., Aug. 31, 1935—The galleries were all rooting for 17-year-old local favorite Patty Berg, but Glenna Collett Vare would not be denied today as she won her sixth Women's National Amateur golf championship on the Interlachen Country Club course in this Minneapolis suburb.

Glenna Collett Vare won six Women's National championships. *UPI*

Berg, a native of Minneapolis who started playing golf only four years ago, went down to defeat as Vare finished with two birdies to go up three holes with two left to play in the 36-hole final round of match play.

For Vare, it was the latest in a collection of national titles that began in 1922. She won again in 1925 and then three straight years, 1928 to 1930.

Most U.S. National Amateur championships: 6, Glenna Collett Vare, Philadelphia, Pennsylvania, 1922, 1925, 1928–30, 1935

Wright On

CHULA VISTA, Cal., July 12, 1964—Mickey Wright sank a seven-foot birdie putt on the 16th hole to take over the lead and hold on for a playoff victory in the U.S. Women's Open today.

Wright and Ruth Jessen were tied at 290 yesterday after 72 holes on the 6,400-yard San Diego Country Club course. Her birdie putt on the 16th enabled Wright to finish with 70, two strokes better than Jessen in the 18-hole playoff.

The victory for the 29-year-old Wright—her fourth in the U.S. Open—brought her first-prize money of $2,200. Wright is the second woman to win four Opens, the first being Betsy Rawls in 1951, 1953, 1957, and 1960.

Most U.S. Women's Open golf championships: 4, Mickey Wright, 1958–59, 1961, 1964 (Ties Betsy Rawls, 1951, 1953, 1957, 1960)

Double Eagle from Taiwan

BIRMINGHAM, Mich., June 13, 1985—Tze-Chung Chen, a 27-year-old golfer from Taiwan who didn't take up the game until he was 17, made history today in the first round of the U.S. Open at the Oakland Hills Country Club.

Taking aim at the second green on his second shot, 255 yards from the pin on the par-5 of 527 yards, he hit it perfect for a double eagle, the first ever recorded in the 84-year history of the Open.

T.C., as he is called, ended up with a 5-under-par 65 that gave him the first-round lead. "I feel great and so surprised," Chen said. "I never did it before."

Most double eagles, U.S. Open: 1, Tze-Chung Chen, June 13, 1985, Birmingham, Mich.

The Golden Bear

AUGUSTA, Ga., April 13, 1986—He was considered past his prime, but 46-year-old Jack Nicklaus won his sixth Masters today with one of the most dramatic finishes in the history of golf.

With a spectacular charge over the last 10 holes (7-under-par 33 from No. 9 through No. 18), Nicklaus ended up with a 9-under 279 and a one-stroke triumph over Greg Norman and Tom Kite. The Golden Bear thus broke his own record of five Masters victories.

Nobody in golf history has won more major tournament titles (20) than Nicklaus. He shares the record for most PGA championships (5) with Walter Hagen, and he shares the record for most U.S. Open championships (4) with Ben Hogan, Bobby Jones, and Willie Anderson. And he holds the record for lowest score in a U.S. Open (272).

Most Masters tournament victories: 6, Jack Nicklaus, 1963, 1965, 1966, 1972, 1975, 1986

Most PGA championships: 5, Jack Nicklaus, 1963, 1971, 1973, 1975, 1980 (Ties Walter Hagen, 1921, 1924–27)

Most U.S. Open championships: 4, Jack Nicklaus, 1962, 1967, 1972, 1980 (Ties Bobby Jones, 1923, 1926, 1929, 1930; and Willie Anderson, 1901, 1903–5)

Most victories, major tournaments: 20, Jack Nicklaus (6 Masters, 5 PGA, 4 U.S. Open, 3 British Open, 2 U.S. Amateur)

Lowest Score, U.S. Open: 272, Jack Nicklaus, 1980

Jack Nicklaus hits out of the rough in the fourth of his six Masters championships. *UPI*

Teen Tiger

PONTE VEDRA, Fla., Aug. 28, 1994—Eighteen-year-old Tiger Woods staged the greatest comeback in the 99-year history of the U.S. Amateur Golf Championship today to become the tournament's youngest champion.

The teen-ager from Cypress, Cal., was six down to Trip Kuehne with 12 holes to play in the 36-hole showdown and he battled back for a 1-up victory.

A three-time U.S. junior boys champion, Woods became the first black to win the Amateur and his victory earned invitations to the 1995 Masters and U.S. and British Opens.

Youngest winner, U.S. Amateur Golf Championship: Tiger Woods, 18

Tiger Woods was the youngest to cop the U.S. Amateur Championship.   *Wide World*

TENNIS

Rod's Slams

NEW YORK, Sept. 8, 1969—Rod Laver beat fellow Australian Tony Roche, 7–9, 6–1, 6–2, 6–2, to win the U.S. Open championship at the West Side Tennis Club in Forest Hills today and became the first man ever to complete two tennis grand slams.

The lefthanded Laver duplicated his feat of 1962 when, as an amateur, he won the singles titles at the Australian, French, Wimbledon, and U.S. Open tournaments. This year the 31-year-old Aussie is a pro and earned $16,000 for the U.S. title.

Rod Laver makes the get as he downs Tony Roche to win the U.S. Open and complete the second of his grand slams in 1969.   *UPI*

The only other man to win a grand slam was American Don Budge, who achieved the honor as an amateur in 1938.

Most tennis grand slams: 2, Rod Laver, 1962, 1969

Margaret Smith Court defeats Rosemary Casals in the U.S. Open in 1970 to match Maureen Connolly's grand slam. *UPI*

Court's Court

FOREST HILLS, N.Y., Sept. 8, 1973—Billie Jean King calls her "The Arm" because of her incredible reach. And Margaret Smith Court reached new heights today when she vanquished Evonne Goolagong, 7–6, 5–7, 6–2, in an all-Australian final to win the U.S. Open Championship.

The ageless 31-year-old powerhouse thus extended her record to 24 Grand Slam singles titles, five more than runner-up Helen Wills Moody, who achieved the last of her 19 at Wimbledon in 1938.

In 1970 Smith Court became the second woman to complete a grand slam when she defeated Rosemary Casals at the U.S. Open. Her sweep of the four major titles duplicated the feat of Maureen "Little Mo" Connolly in 1953.

Most Grand Slam singles titles: 24, Margaret Smith Court (Australian, 1960–66, 1969–71, 1973; French, 1962, 1964, 1969–70, 1973; Wimbledon, 1963, 1965, 1970; U.S., 1962, 1965, 1969, 1970, 1973)

Most Grand Slams: 1, Margaret Court Smith, 1970 (Ties Maureen Connolly, 1953)

Boom Boom at Wimbledon

WIMBLEDON, England, July 7, 1985—Defying tradition and logic that said he was too young to win, 17-year-old Boris Becker of West Germany captured the Wimbledon's men's singles title today.

Boris Becker was only 17 when he won the Wimbledon crown in 1985.   *Wide World*

Boom Boom, as he is nicknamed for good reason, trounced 27-year-old Kevin Curren of the United States, 6–3, 6–7, 7–6, 6–4, to become the youngest champion in the 109-year history of the event.

His triumph also made him the first unseeded player to win and the first German male Wimbledon champion.

Youngest Wimbledon singles champion, men: 17, Boris Becker, 1985

Martina's Destiny

WIMBLEDON, England, July 7, 1990—In each of the last two Wimbledon finals Martina Navratilova was frustrated by Germany's Steffi Graf in her quest for a record ninth All-England (Wimbledon) title.

Today, however, Martina easily dominated Zina Garrison of the United States, 6–4, 6–1, to take sole possession of the mark she had shared at eight with Helen Wills Moody of the United States.

"There are some records that may never be broken," she said. "Joe DiMaggio's hitting streak, Hank Aaron's home-run record. This was one that was within reach."

The 33-year-old Navratilova, who defected from Czechoslovakia in 1975, also has the record for most consecutive Wimbledon titles (6).

Most Wimbledon singles titles: 9, Martina Navratilova, 1978, 1979, 1982, 1983, 1984, 1985, 1986, 1987, 1990
Most consecutive Wimbledon singles titles: 6, 1982–87

Cannon Serve

FLUSHING, N.Y., Sept. 9, 1990—Pete Sampras, a low-key Californian with booming 120-mile-per-hour serves, demolished flamboyant Andre Agassi today to become the youngest men's champion in U.S. Open history.

The unheralded 19-year-old Sampras, ranked No. 81 less than a year ago, fired 13 aces and added 12 more

Martina Navratilova captured her ninth Wimbledon title in 1990.
Wide World

service winners in the 6–4, 6–3, 6–2 rout of his 20-year-old fellow American.

Just 28 days past his 19th birthday, Sampras entered the record book in place of Oliver Campbell, who was 19 years, six months when he won the Open 100 years ago, in 1890.

"I'm just a normal 19-year-old with an unusual job,

doing unusual things, like I did today," said Sampras, whose feat earned him $350,000.

"It was an old-fashioned street mugging," summed up the vanquished Agassi.

Youngest U.S. Open champion, men: Pete Sampras, 19 years, 28 days, 1990

Pete Sampras scores one of his 13 aces as he routs Andre Agassi to become the youngest U.S. Open champion in 1990.   *Wide World*

A Modern Queen

FLUSHING, N.Y., Sept. 9, 1995—In a stirring renewal of their rivalry, Steffi Graf won the U.S. Open championship today, defeating the comebacking Monica Seles, 7–6 (8–6), 0–6, 6–3.

For Seles it was a tearful finish after spending 28 months in limbo as a result of being stabbed by a deranged German man who had wanted Seles out of the way so Graf could be No. 1 in the world again.

For Graf it was her fourth U.S. Open title as the 26-year-old German upped her career edge to 7–4 over her Yugoslavian-born 21-year-old opponent.

It was also Graf's 18th Grand Slam singles title, putting her in the record book as the first woman to win at least four of each of the Grand Slam singles titles.

Four or more titles in Grand Slam events: Steffi Graf (U.S. Open, 1988–89, 1993, 1995; Australian, 1988–90, 1994–95; French, 1987–88, 1993, 1995; Wimbledon, 1988–89, 1991–93, 1995)

Steffi Graf captured her fourth U.S. Open title in 1995.   *Wide World*

HORSE RACING

Half-Dozen Roses

LOUISVILLE, Ky., May 3, 1952—"Plain Ben" Jones led a parade of familiar faces to the winner's circle today after 11–10 favorite Hill Gail won the 78th running of the Kentucky Derby. The race was televised coast-to-coast for the first time.

This was the sixth time Jones had tightened the girth on a Derby winner, a record number of victories among trainers. It was also the fifth time Eddie Arcaro had ridden the winner. And it was the fifth time a Calumet Farm horse had won. Mrs. Warren Wright, widow of the Calumet owner, accepted the trophy.

The race itself was not without its suspense, for Hill Gail—who broke from the inside post position—swerved to the outside shortly after the start. After about a half mile, though, Arcaro got a hold on the horse and kept him in front for the remainder of the mile-and-a-quarter classic to finish two lengths in front of Sub Fleet, owned by Charles T. Fisher's Dixiana Farm.

Jones, the grand old man of Derby Racing, saddled Triple Crown winners Whirlaway in 1941 and Citation in 1948, as well as Lawrin in 1938, Pensive in 1944 and Ponder in 1949.

Most Kentucky Derby winners, trainer: 6, Ben Jones—1938, Lawrin; 1941, Whirlaway; 1944, Pensive; 1948, Citation; 1949, Ponder; and 1952, Hill Gail

Trainer Ben Jones, with his sixth Kentucky Derby winner, Hill Gail, ridden by Eddie Arcaro, in 1952.   *UPI*

Majestic Hartack

LOUISVILLE, Ky., May 3, 1969—Undefeated Majestic Prince, out of California, and Arts and Letters, out of New York, helped draw the first 100,000-plus crowd into Churchill Downs for today's 95th Kentucky Derby.

When it was over, President Richard Nixon and 106, 332 others had seen Majestic Prince, ridden by Bill Hartack, engage Arts and Letters, ridden by Braulio Baeza, at the quarter pole and race almost as one to the wire, where Majestic Prince earned the decision by a neck.

The victory for Hartack was his fifth in the Derby, matching the record number of triumphs by Eddie Arcaro. At the same time, trainer Johnny Longden, who rode Count Fleet to victory here in 1943, became the first man to have both ridden and saddled a Derby winner.

Most Kentucky Derby winners, jockey: 5, Bill Hartack—1957, Iron Leige; 1960, Venetian Way; 1962, Decidedly; 1964, Northern Dancer; and 1969, Majestic Prince (Ties Eddie Arcaro—1938, Lawrin; 1941, Whirlaway; 1945, Hoop Jr.; 1948, Citation; and 1952, Hill Gail)

Record Ride

LAUREL, Md., Dec. 31, 1974—One year ago today, an 18-year-old boy was in the stands at Laurel Race Course watching Sandy Hawley ride a horse to victory for the 515th time in 1973. Never in thoroughbred history had any jockey been aboard more than 500 winners in a calendar year, and Hawley established a record that many observers felt would stand for years to come.

One of those who agreed was the 18-year-old, Chris McCarron, who was willing to "bet anything that Sandy's record will stand for 20 years." McCarron was a qualified observer since his older brother Gregg was a jockey, and he himself worked as a stable hand at the racetrack.

A month after Hawley's 515th, McCarron received his jockey's license and rode his first horse late in January. On Feb. 9 of this year, young Chris rode the first winner of his life. By Dec. 17, just two weeks ago, McCarron rode Ohmylove to a neck victory, beating a horse ridden by brother Gregg. The trip to the winner's circle was the 516th for young McCarron, breaking the less-than-year-old mark established by Hawley.

Chris is an apprentice rider, receiving an advantage in the weight his horses must carry because of his inexperience. But what he lacks in experience, he makes up in ability. Once he realized the record was within his reach, he began riding seven days a week. He rode here in Maryland Monday through Saturday, and on Sundays traveled to Penn National course near Harrisburg, Pa. He became only the second rider to surpass the 500 victory mark in one year. Then he broke the all-time record.

Chris McCarron, 18, rode 546 winners in 1974.   *UPI*

In today's seventh race, on the last day of the year, he rode Sarah Percy to victory in the feature race. The mare was a 3 to 5 favorite, and McCarron made the chalk players happy by bringing her home three and a half lengths in front for his 546th victory of the year.

Most winners, year, jockey: 546, Chris McCarron, 1974

Master in the Saddle

HALLANDALE, Fla, Jan. 20, 1990—Bill Shoemaker urged Beau Genius home through a narrow opening today to score a nose victory in the Hallandale Handicap at Gulfstream Park.

It was the last of Shoemaker's three rides and his only winning effort as the 58-year-old jockey winds down a career in which he has won more races than any other rider in history.

For several months now, Shoemaker has been barnstorming around the country for crowds who wanted to see the 4-foot 11-inch, 97 pounder who has been riding since he was an 18-year-old apprentice in 1949. Four years ago, at age 54, he became the oldest jockey ever to win the Kentucky Derby when he brought Ferdinand

Bill Shoemaker, aboard Ferdinand, won his fourth Kentucky Derby as a 54-year-old in 1986.   *Wide World*

home to victory at Churchill Downs. It was his fourth Derby triumph.

In today's 7-furlong feature, Shoemaker kept Beau Genius near to the pace as the six-horse field stayed closely bunched into the stretch. With about 70 yards left to the finish line, Shoemaker took advantage of an opening to rush past front-runners Shuttleman and Norquestor, and finished a nose in front of the fast-closing The Red Rolls.

Beau Genius paid $9.80 to win, but many of the fans holding winning tickets were expected to keep them as souvenirs, particularly if this turns out to be Shoemaker's last winning ride.

Shoemaker, who has more than 40,000 mounts and 8,833 winners to his credit, will ride only one more race in his career. The largely ceremonial farewell appearance will come in a nationally televised race from Santa Anita Park in Arcadia, Cal., on Feb. 3, 1990.

Most winners, career, jockey: Bill Shoemaker, 8,833, 1949–90

Victory Cigar

ELMONT, N.Y., Oct. 28, 1995—Allen Paulson's Cigar roared to victory in the $3-million Breeders Cup Classic at Belmont Park today, earning $1.56 million and boosting his winnings for the season to a record $4.8 million. That broke the mark of $4.5 million set by Sunday Silence in 1989.

With regular rider Jerry Bailey in the irons, the 3–5 Cigar took the lead at the head of the stretch and drove home to win by two lengths ahead of 51-to-1 shot L'Carriere. His time for the 10-furlongs was 1:59 2/5, nearly a second better than the old mark. The five-year-old Cigar notched his 10th victory in 10 starts this year and his 13th straight victory overall. This bettered Spectacular Bid's 9-for-9 streak in 1980.

Cigar didn't run in any Triple Crown races as a 3-year-old and had a rather undistinguished career until late last year when trainer Billy Mott stopped running him on the turf and switched him to dirt courses. Among the eight Grade I stakes Cigar won this year are the Meadowlands Cup, the Molson Million, the Hollywood Gold Cup, the Woodward, and the Jockey Club Gold Cup.

Most money won by a thoroughbred, one year: $4,819,800, Cigar, 1995

Cigar, with Jerry Bailey up, hit the jackpot when he won the Breeders Cup Classic in 1995.   *Wide World*

Krone's Alone

NEW YORK, Nov. 15, 1995—Julie Krone rode three winners at Aqueduct Race Course today, passing a major milestone by winning the 3,000th race of her 15-year-career. The 32-year-old jockey brought home the favored Pleasant Court in the first race before booting in 2-to-1 shot Dustin's Dream in the fourth race for

Julie Krone, atop Colonial Affair, won the Belmont Stakes in 1993.
Wide World

No. 3,000 and later won the sixth race aboard Book of Fortune, who paid $6.30.

The 4-foot 10½-inch native of Benton Harbor, Mich., was the first woman to win a riding title at a major track when she was the winningest jockey at both Monmouth Park and Meadowlands racetracks in New Jersey in 1987.

She was also the first woman to ride a winner in a Triple Crown race when she brought home Colonial Affair ahead of the field in the 1993 Belmont Stakes.

It was just three months ago that Krone rode in six races at Saratoga in upstate New York before exchanging her silks and tack for a wedding gown. In an evening ceremony, she married Matthew Muzikar, a 6-foot 4-inch, 215-pound security guard at the racetrack.

Two summers ago Krone rode five winners in one day at Saratoga, tying the record set by Angel Cordero, Jr., July 31, 1968 and equaled by Ron Turcotte, Aug. 7, 1973. Ten days later she fractured her ankle in a fall, an injury that sidelined her for almost a year.

First female jockey to ride 3,000 winners: Julie Krone, Nov. 15, 1995

AUTO RACING

Ageless at Indy

INDIANAPOLIS, Ind., May 24, 1987—Al Unser Sr. raced home five seconds in front of Roberto Guerrero and into the record books with his fourth victory today in the Indianapolis 500.

Just five days short of his 48th birthday, Unser is the oldest driver ever to win the event. After victories in 1970, 1971 and 1977, today's triumph ties him with A. J. Foyt Jr. for most victories in the Memorial Day classic.

Probably the happiest loser in the race was Unser's 25-year-old son, Al, Jr., who finished fourth. And Al,

Al Unser heads down the main straightaway en route to his fourth Indy 500 victory in 1987.   *Wide World*

Sr.'s brother, Bobby, who had previously been the oldest winner of the race, was handling broadcast chores for the nationally televised race.

Unser was lucky to be in the race at all. As recently as 11 days ago he was a driver without a car. The neon-yellow Penski March–Cosworth was supposed to be driven by Danny Ongais, but he crashed during a practice run and race officials said he had not sufficiently recovered from a concussion to drive today.

Unser averaged 162.147 miles per hour in taking 3 hours, 4 minutes and 59.147 seconds to complete the 200 trips around the two-and-a-half-mile oval.

Most victories, Indianapolis 500: 4, Al Unser Sr., 1970, 1971, 1978, 1987 (Ties A. J. Foyt Jr., 1961, 1964, 1967, 1977)
Oldest driver to win the Indianapolis 500: Al Unser Sr., 1987, 47 years, 11 months, 25 days

Flying Dutchman

INDIANAPOLIS, Ind., May 27, 1990—Arie Luyendyk blew past Bobby Rahal with 32 laps to go and was never headed as he went on to win the Indianapolis 500 in the fastest time ever.

Driving a 1990 Lola-Chevy, Luyendyk averaged 185.984 miles per hour to shatter the previous mark of 170.222 set by Rahal in 1986. Luyendyk, born in Sommelsdyk, Holland, but now living in Brookfield, Wis., needed just 2 hours, 41 minutes and 18.248 seconds to complete the 200 laps.

Rahal was 10.7 seconds behind, averaging 185.778 m.p.h. Defending champion Emerson Fittipaldi, who led for 128 laps, experienced tire problems late in the race, but still managed to finish third with an average speed of 185.185.

It was the first Indy-car victory for the 36-year-old Luyendyk after seven years and 77 starts.

Fastest average time, Indianapolis 500: 185.984 m.p.h., Arie Luyendyk, May 27, 1990

SWIMMING

Spitz's Spritz

MUNICH, West Germany, Sept. 4, 1972—Mark Spitz picked up his seventh Olympic gold medal tonight as he swam the butterfly leg on the winning United States 400-meter medley relay team. And for the seventh time in these Olympic Games, the 22-year-old Spitz was in on a world record.

A native of California who attended Indiana University, Spitz also set world marks in the individual 100- and 200-meter freestyle events, the 100- and 200-meter butterfly races, and in anchoring the winning 400-meter and 800-meter freestyle relay teams.

The 6-foot, 160-pound Spitz—whose extraordinarily long legs enable him to kick deeper in the water than

Mark Spitz butterflies his way to a seventh Olympic gold medal in 1972.   *UPI*

most swimmers—is the first individual to win seven gold medals in a single Olympic Games. Three others had won as many as five, but no one had ever won more than that.

Most gold medals, one Olympics: 7, Mark Spitz, United States, 1972

CYCLING

An American in Paris

PARIS, France, July 22, 1990—"I think this is the toughest sport in the world," Greg LeMond said today after sweeping down the Champs-Elysee to again win the Tour de France.

Few would argue with the 29-year-old from Wayzata, Minn., who became the first American to capture the world's most prestigious bicycle race in 1986.

While not as dramatic as his second victory in 1989, when his margin was eight seconds, this was LeMond's third triumph in the grueling 23-day, 2,542-mile test on a course that includes the Alps and the Pyrenees.

LeMond's 1989 victory marked an inspirational comeback following a hunting accident in which he was shot by his brother-in-law and, beyond that, later, underwent surgery for a shin injury.

His goal is to match and surpass the Tour de France record of five victories held by Jacques Anquetil, Eddy Merckx, and Bernard Hinault.

Most Tour de France victories by an American: 3, Greg LeMond

Greg LeMond cycles to his third triumph in the Tour de France in 1990.   *Wide World*

SPEED SKATING

SPEED SKATING

Sweep on Ice

LAKE PLACID, N.Y., Feb. 24, 1980—He'd already
_____ _____ dal in Olympic record time at 500
_____ 5,000 _____ and ____ times he'd gon

Sweep on Ice

LAKE PLACID, N.Y. Feb. 23, 1980—He'd already won four gold medals in Olympic-record time at 500 meters, 1,000, 1,500, and 5,000. And now Eric Heiden was at the starting line for the 10,000-meter speed-skating race, the most grueling of all, in the Winter Olympic Games.

The 21-year-old from Madison, Wis., proceeded to go faster today than anyone on speed skates ever has for 10,000 meters. He broke the world record by six seconds (14:28.13) as he skated to an unprecedented fifth gold medal, the most anyone has ever achieved in a Winter Olympics.

Most gold medals, one Winter Olympics: 5, Eric Heiden, 500 meters, 1,000, 1,500, 5,000, 10,000, Feb. 15–23, 1980

Eric Heiden won five Olympic gold medals at Lake Placid in 1980.
UPI

SOCCER

Boot Marathon

SEATTLE, Wash., Dec. 15, 1985—The teams were scoreless after 90 minutes of regulation time in the NCAA championship soccer game today between UCLA and American University at the Kingdome. Nobody scored in the first overtime. They went into a second overtime . . . a third . . . a fourth . . . a fifth . . . a sixth . . . a seventh. Still scoreless.

Prior to the eighth overtime, UCLA assistant coach Steve Sampson pleaded with his weary players: "Get out there and finish this thing so we can go home."

With 3:55 left in the eighth overtime, UCLA sophomore Paul Burke broke through American's defense and booted a shot from 13 yards to beat the goalie.

It was finally over, with UCLA winning the longest soccer game in collegiate history.

Longest game: 8 overtimes, 2 hours, 46 minutes, 5 seconds, UCLA vs. American University, Dec. 15, 1985

BOATING

Racing the Atlantic

NEWPORT, R.I., June 15, 1988—It was more than another victory today for Philippe Poupon, a 33-year-old Frenchman, in the Carlsberg Single-Handed Trans-Atlantic Race.

Competing in the 3,000–mile voyage from Plymouth, England, Poupon made it in 10 days, 9 hours, 15 minutes for the fastest passage of any sailboat, single-handed or crewed, across the Atlantic from East to West.

His 60-foot trimaran, *Fleury Michon,* averaged more than 13 knots and Poupon cut more than six days off the 16-day, 12-hour record he set in the same race in 1984.

Fastest Trans-Atlantic passage in a sailboat, single-handed or crewed, East to West: 10 days, 9 hours, 15 minutes, Philippe Poupon, 1988

Pedaling Across the Sea

PLYMOUTH HARBOR, England, July 24, 1992—As a member of the British Coast Guard put it, "A bloody wally on a bicycle is pedaling across the pond."

Indeed, Dwight Collins of Noroton, Conn., pedaled a 24-foot boat across the Atlantic Ocean, arriving today in 40 days, a record for the fastest human-powered craft. The old mark of 56 days was set in a rowboat in 1954.

The 34-year-old Collins, a real-estate agent, survived on a daily diet of freeze-dried food and an occasional beer. In the process he lost 30 pounds.

His covered boat was made of cedar strips and carbon fiber.

"I didn't expect to get here so quickly," Collins said. "The weather was worse than I expected, so gale after gale catapulted me across."

Fastest passage, U.S. to England, human-powered craft: 40 days, Dwight Collins, 1992

This is the boat that Dwight Collins pedaled across the Atlantic in 1992.   *Wide World*

Around the World in 80 Days

LA BAULE, France, April 20, 1993—More than a century after Jules Verne wrote *Around the World in 80 Days,* five sailors fulfilled the writer's imagination in a catamaran.

After sailing more than 27,000 nautical miles, skipper Bruno Peyron of France and his four-man crew finished their nonstop journey tonight, precisely 79 days, 6 hours, 20 minutes, and 50 seconds after departure.

Three other Frenchmen—Oliver Despaignes, Marc Vallin, and Jacques Vincent—and American Cam Lewis shared the voyage in Peyron's 86-foot *Commodore Explorer*. They beat the record for a sailboat of 109 days, 8 hours, set in 1990 by a Frenchman, Titouan Lamazou, in a monohull.

A collision with two sperm whales that resulted in a cracked hull north of the Equator could not keep skipper and crew from achieving an impossible dream.

Fastest sailboat passage around the world: 80 days, Bruno Peyron, Oliver Despaignes, Marc Vallin, Cam Lewis, 1993

SLED-DOG
RACING

They Did It at Iditarod

NOME, Alaska, March 11, 1992—A Swiss-born musher who sings to his dogs won the 1,159-mile Iditarod Trail Sled Dog Race in record time today.

His arrival hailed by blaring sirens and cheering spectators in this Gold Rush town on the Bering Sea coast, Martin Buser stopped his sled beneath a wooden arch on Front Street that marks the end of the "Last Great Race on Earth."

Despite being on their feet most of time, Buser and his dogs seemed almost as fresh as when they left Anchorage on Feb. 29. "The dogs kept getting stronger and stronger," Buser said. "I was just the lucky guy who was driving."

Buser came in some 10 hours ahead of his nearest rival. His elapsed time of 10 days, 19 hours, 17 minutes slashed about six hours off the 1990 record set by four-time winner Susan Butcher.

In addition to the $50,000 first prize, Buser won a pickup truck valued at $25,000. The dog's reward? They no longer had to listen to Buser's singing.

Fastest time, Iditarod Trail Sled-Dog Race: 10 days, 19 hours, 17 minutes, Martin Buser, 1992.

ABOUT THE AUTHORS

Zander Hollander is president of Associated Features Inc., specialists in sports publishing. He is coauthor of *The Sports Nostalgia Quiz Book* series, edits *The Complete Handbook of Baseball, Pro Football,* and *Pro Basketball*, and has edited six sports encyclopedias, most recently *Bud Collins' Modern Encyclopedia of Tennis*. He was a sportswriter on the late *New York World-Telegram and Sun.*

David Schulz, coauthor of *The Sports Nostalgia Quiz Book* series and *The Counter-Terrorism Handbook,* has written other books on sports, travel, and leisure-oriented activities. He has been a contributing editor to *Fodor's Travel Guides,* the *Birnbaum Travel Guides,* and the 20-volume *The Ocean World of Jacques Cousteau,* several sports encyclopedias, and short-story collections. He wrote sports for the Associated Press and was a staffer on *The Morning Telegraph.*

Revised and updated FOURTH EDITION
with more than 60
new record-breaking stories!

THE ILLUSTRATED
SPORTS RECORD BOOK

Zander Hollander and David Schulz

Setting the record straight, here in a single book
are more than 400 records re-created in more than
200 stories. Sports immortals and their feats abound—
Cal Ripken, Jr., Michael Jordan, Steffi Graf, Joe
DiMaggio, Wayne Gretzky, Muhammad Ali, Jack
Nicklaus ... and many more. Perfect for settling
living-room or bar-room debates, this fourth edition
is illustrated with more than 100 action photos.

* Prices slightly higher in Canada   (0-451-18858-6—$5.99)